Clearing Space for Grace

Finding New Life After Loss

R. Joan McDermott

©2022

9/28/2022

Shirby!

I hope you enjoy my little book and also get something out of it. Love
Jan

ISBN: 979-8814528056

Edited and formatted by Pam Van Allen, Whizzits Publishing

"The Peace Prayer of St. Francis" translated from the French by Pam Van Allen

---

Clearing Space for Grace/R. Joan McDermott

Summary: Memoir of a woman who entered the convent of the Sisters of Mercy as a teen, left the order in her thirties, married, divorced, and recovered from alcoholism through her religious faith.

1. Memoir. 2. Self-help—Healing Through Spirituality. 3. Mental Health Issues—Alcohol Use Disorder. 4. Women's Issues—Rape 5. Self-Improvement

THE PEACE PRAYER OF ST. FRANCIS

Lord, make me an instrument of your peace.
Where hate grows, let me plant love.
Where offense grows, let me plant forgiveness.
Where discord grows, let me plant unity.
Where error grows, let me plant the truth.

Where doubt grows, let me plant faith.
Where despair grows, let me plant hope.
Where darkness grows, let me cast your light.
Where there is sadness, let me sow joy.

Oh Master, may I not seek so much.
May I comfort more than I am
   comforted.
May I understand more than I am
   understood.
May I love others more than I am
   loved.

Because it is by giving that one
   receives.
It is by forgetting oneself that one
   finds the light.
It is by forgiving others that one is forgiven.
It is by dying that one is resurrected to eternal life.

DEDICATION

I dedicate this book to my wonderful parents. Their undying love for each other, their personal love for God, and their devoted care for us—all their priceless gifts of life—have witnessed to me the true meaning of love. Such great Faith, Hope, and Love have been my ever-present inspiration, even to this day.

ACKNOWLEDGEMENTS

Two major shining stars have been most helpful in putting together my life's story and showcasing it to reveal the core message of *Clearing Space for Grace*—finding new life.

First and foremost, my wonderful sensitive editor, Pam Van Allen. So many pieces of my life needed to be put in good order so you, the reader, wouldn't get lost in the telling. The experience of sorting through events as they occurred in my life was so difficult for me. I just couldn't remember. I learned how to find some facts through Google and where to find the photos or certificates that would indicate the sequence of my eighty-five years. I acknowledge her sensitivity and gentle encouragement that kept me moving forward.

None of this would have mattered if Jim Mazrimas had not been with me through the process of getting all this information on the computer and to the right person. Jim's continual question to me was, "How can I help?" He gave so much of his time and dedication to the project as I accomplished each of my tasks.

Of course, I want to acknowledge my supportive friends and their encouragement and joy in what I wanted to achieve.

I bestow my great gratitude upon one and all who inspire me to show up to life with loving presence and joy.

NOTE FROM THE AUTHOR

ဟာလာလာလာ

Memoirs are neither novels nor histories. They are a person's life as they recall living it. I'm sure I didn't get all the names, places, or dates right. But that's not the important part of my story. What I want to impart about my life were the lessons I learned from my experiences. My most important truth was that God's grace is found in the most unexpected places, often coming to me following a devastating loss.

In some cases, I've left out my friends and relatives' names. This was purposeful. In other cases, the names are right there for you to read and remember.

Like most people, my life has had its ups and downs. I know that without those downs, I wouldn't have had the most important awakenings that led me to write this book. Thank you so much for reading.

R. Joan McDermott
2022

TABLE OF CONTENTS

ഔൽഔൽഔൽ

INTRODUCTION

The truth crashed in on me. Everything I'd gone through was the necessary catalyst for me to change my life to way I wanted it.

I had lost my home, my health, and any means of financial support. These losses weighed heavily upon me. I needed to lighten the burden of darkness that had crept into my broken heart. The stark realization of my losses had plunged me into a place of emptiness, engulfing me. How could I build on emptiness?

Anger and bitterness threw me into the chokehold of negativity. So much overwhelming emotion became intolerable. This black hole was more than I could bear. It forced me to look my need squarely in the eye. Only by facing it could I let go of what was strangling me.

From the depths of my heart, I cried out for help. Help arrived when I made a frightening and long-delayed decision. I deliberately chose to live in gratitude and joy for everything I had, no matter what I had lost. This commitment to positivity became my daily spiritual practice.

In the early stages of my efforts to reach resolution of my chaos and confusion, I noticed my heavy heart felt a little lighter. I attributed it to my change to a more grateful frame of mind. Only by God's grace was I able to move in this new direction.

Grieving can be a tumultuous process. Each of us moves through it in our own way. For me, coping with the range of emotions and managing the day was difficult. Having a stroke further muddled my thinking.

In July 2020, I experienced a stroke that affected the entire left side of my body. My balance was off and my head seemed foggy. I had to move to a new apartment by the end of August, and the disability caused by the stroke significantly interfered. Luckily, I had good friends to help. A couple of weeks later, the lingering symptoms of the stroke contributed to a bad fall that required hospitalization and therapy. Physically, I was a mess!

The Covid epidemic had erupted. Being isolated seemed to calm my thinking and quiet the negative talk in my head. Surprisingly, it helped me to move forward, to take action, to begin living again. My decision to build on being grateful opened my life wider to new possibilities.

The joy that flows from gratitude emerged. Once I could see my blessings, it was possible to focus on the bounty in my life instead of the lack.

I let go of my resentment and anger over what I had perceived as an unfair loss of an investment. The man who set up a plan for my coaching practice placed me in the wrong program. I'm still paying off that debt. I began to see the part I had played in that whole fiasco. Accepting reality proved to be the resolution of my grief.

The grace that surfaced when all seemed so impossible proved to be the bedrock from which sprang hope, help and healing. As I was writing about my life's experiences, I realized that each time frame, each loss, each surviving of the unnamable traumas, had an element of clearing a space for grace. Whether I use the term clearing space as a noun or a verb, it is an awakening to something new. It woke me up to releasing what was holding me in bondage and moved me forward. Grace, that unmerited gift, had arrived when all seemed lost.

My awareness grew of the beautiful people who were there for me. Daily, they were helping me put my life back together. Their loving service has been paramount for adhering to my inner focus on the positive.

The truth came to me through this clearing of space for grace—I could choose gratitude and joy. I didn't have to. But the alternative was to remain stuck in self-pity and rage. Nor did I want to live in the self-hatred that sickened my heart each time I imagined I was the one who had brought this entire mess on myself.

Taking the time I needed to heal is an essential part of finding new life after loss. I need consistent but gentle daily renewal of my decision to practice gratitude, which requires support and constant reminders. I find this help from my meditations, the readings I choose, and even the movies I watch. I need the lift I get from interactions with my spiritually healthy friends and mentors. One of my writing mentors, Mark Nepo, speaks to me every day from the title and subtitle of his inspirational book—*The Book of Awakening: Having the Life You Want by Being Present to the Life You Have.* What a treat to read his page of the day in my early morning hours.

Tapping, which is termed EFT (Emotional Freedom Technique), is another great tool that connects the mind, body, and spirit as we tap on the meridians. We hold so much emotionality in our bodies that needs to be exposed and released. Tapping is a great way to get in touch with what is holding us in bondage by naming and releasing these emotions.

In contrast with traditional psychotherapy, which requires talking about emotions, tapping is a method people like me can use. I tend to block feeling emotion and have trouble naming what I'm feeling, so that I can't work effectively in verbal therapy. EFT offers a way of moving through to the truth with fewer words by expressing what troubles us in a simple sentence while tapping. It works especially well for freeing me from self-hatred, the spiritual malady that blocks me from healthy self-love.

I hope you will enjoy reading my life's experiences. While writing them, I became more aware of the blessings hidden behind each painful change. As you read, notice the repeating theme of feelings of powerlessness and emptiness just before I find a different way to move on. That is what I call the space of grace. My inner battles were clearing space for the grace to enter so I could be open to new possibilities.

Grace is the undeserved blessing from the Divine all of us receive throughout our lives. Sometimes it's hard to perceive these gifts as blessings until later. Sometimes we never recognize them as blessings, camouflaged by the resentments in our hearts.

Grace is the traffic light that changes unexpectedly or the new friend from church. Grace is your sister forgiving you for a wrong. Grace is the smile of a stranger. Grace is the gratitude in our own heart.

All my struggling and grappling were, in

fact, helping me to let go of what I couldn't change. Finding new life after my losses continues to promote growth into greater authenticity. A world of peace, gratitude, and joy is always waiting for me when I persevere. It takes grit and the ability to make better choices.

After all these years, I am happy to say I can count on this process of grieving. It is imperfect and messy, but so worth the journey inward and onward. Of the many tools I have discovered in the movement to new beginnings is the priceless gift of breathing slowly and deliberately through the passage of change. May you be blessed in your discovery of the unmerited, God-given, grace that gives rise to the gratitude, peace, and joy of renewed life.

Bill and Alice McDermott--Mother and Father

Chapter 1 — AND SO IT BEGINS

ಬಂಞಬಂಞಬಂಞ

The doctor told my mother that she would die if she had a baby. She and my father had tried for a while to have their first child, and it was not happening for them. Ma had just recovered from the last of her three miscarriages. In tears, she told the priest that the doctor said she could die if they continued trying to have a child. He assured her she needn't worry because they could use the rhythm method of birth control. That was a small measure of comfort to her broken heart, but they tried using the rhythm method.

Our mother gave birth almost every year after that. This seemed to prove both the doctor and the priest were wrong. She didn't die, and the rhythm method didn't work. My parents confusing the non-fertile days with the fertile days had something to do with this shocking outcome. They tried to do everything according to the instructions and believed it was the right way.

I find this to be so revealing and so in

keeping with my own experiences. When I do what I believe is the right thing, even if it turns out to be a poor decision, that element of faith steps in to bring about the blessing that flows from the pure intention of my heart. Holding a

Twelve of the fourteen of us and our parents

Alice McDermott
Sister

Leo McDermott
Brother

24

pure intention for me has always meant doing what I believed was God's loving desire that I do. Letting go of the outcome was the key lesson I learned as my loving relationship grew with the God of my heart.

Ma's intention was pure, and she ended up having all the babies she ever wanted. I am so glad she wanted me. On October 5, 1936, Alice and Bill McDermott welcomed a brand-new baby girl, their thirteenth child. They named me Rosemary Joan. There was joy in the family of nine boys and three girls. Two years later, my baby brother was born. He was the fourteenth and completed our family. Since I was still the "baby girl," I had a special status in the family, and my brothers and sisters spoiled me and showed me off. I loved singing and dancing and enjoyed the applause and hugs from my audience. Could my people-pleasing ways have originated this long ago?

But all that attention faded. Sadness crept into my heart when I found everybody gone. My brothers and sisters were either married, working, or at school. I made mud pies in the backyard while Ma checked on me from the pantry window. I grew bored with the mud pies. Sometimes Ma's attention was taken up with her new baby boy. I believe my creativity and curiosity blossomed out of boredom.

I discovered a whole new world around the corner. In those days we had ice boxes, not refrigerators. The homemaker would place a three-to five-pound block of ice in a compartment inside the wooden ice box to keep the food cold.

1940s Ice Box

We bought the ice that kept our food from spoiling at an ice house around the corner. My family's name for it was the "ice lot," because it had abandoned cars and trucks sitting there, inviting me to climb into them. It was great fun to wiggle behind the steering wheel of a big truck and pretend I was driving. As queen of the road, I ruled the imaginary world before me. To get to the ice lot, I only had to walk around the corner and past a few houses, never even crossing the street.

Walking to my sister Patsy's school was different. I was probably five years old. I remember getting the bright idea to walk to her school to visit her. I can't remember how I knew the way. After crossing busy city streets, I found the big, beautiful Tyler School, on a main thoroughfare of the city. Nuns watched boys and girls outside playing during recess. I caught sight of Patsy and waved and called to her. She walked toward me with a disgruntled expression.

One of the nuns approached to invite me inside the school. Oh, how I loved the smell of the newly varnished floors. They glistened in the sunlight coming through the doors and windows as we walked toward the nun's office. My heels clacked on the solid wood.

The sister sat down behind a big desk and took my hand. "What's your name, my dear?"

"Rosemary Joan, but I'm called Joan."

"Well, Joan. It's so nice of you to want to visit your sister at her school."

I smiled at the friendly nun. "I missed her because I'm home with my little brother all day and he can hardly talk yet."

"But, Joan, I know where your family lives. I have to tell you that it's very dangerous for a little girl your age to walk so far alone and cross so many busy streets. You need a grown-up with you to do that."

I held my head high, "Sister, I know how to look both ways before I cross a street."

She smiled, though now I hardly think my proud declaration was reassuring. Sister Mary Eucharia, the nun who served as Tyler School's principal, gave Patsy permission to take me home that day. Ma was shocked at what I had done and gave me a good scolding. She sternly warned me never to do it again.

I would like to interject a bit about my sister Patsy. She is the next oldest to me in the lineup of my siblings. I was so different from her, but she emerged as my protector. My personality as a child was more like a girly-girl, and she was a bit of a tomboy. Nobody at school pushed me around because Patsy would stand up for me. She was able to thwart other students from doing harm to me by using her voice and not her fists. Her typical approach was to step up to the person who was messing with me and shout, "You want a punch in the mouth, kid?" That's all it took to set them running because all the kids knew her reputation.

One day I asked her to teach me how to fight. We set up a meeting in the wide hallway between the bedrooms on the second floor of our house. My elderly grandmother lived with us at that time. Her bedroom was right off the hallway we had chosen for the fighting lesson.

"Okay, this is what you do," Patsy told me. "Put up your dukes. You don't scratch or pull hair, you punch!"

With that proclamation, she showed me what she meant. I danced around trying to avoid her fists.

"Punch." she yelled, ``Punch."

I started punching away. Half the time I had my eyes closed and missed her body completely. We heard our Grandma calling to us in her French-Canadian accent, "Tut, tut, tut. No fight, no fight."

We dropped our fists, stepped into her room, and stood by her bed, to which she was confined. I tried to soothe my grandmother's fears. "It's all right Grandma, Patsy is just teaching me how to fight."

"No fight, no fight," was her response. We stayed with her a little while so she would know we were all right. That was the end of my fighting lessons. Boy, was I glad of that. This fighting business was too rough on my delicate body.

One of my favorite memories from my childhood was getting together with the family on rainy Sundays. Pa had great ideas for entertainment. He let us younger ones stand on the kitchen table and sing a song, do a dance, or recite a poem. We had to do it with poise—no silliness allowed. If we did well, we would be rewarded with an orange slice. It was great fun. I believe the fact that many of us became entertainers later on in life was an outgrowth of these "self-entertaining" Sundays.

The McDermott Family After Mass

Pa introduced another form of entertainment that I loved even more. Sometimes, after Mass on Sundays, we would have an enormous breakfast. My big brothers would come with their wives and children. Seeing all of them was a treat. After everyone left, and we settled down, Ma and Pa would choose some records to play on the Victrola, and we would dance to the music. The family members took turns dancing with each other. I liked dancing with my mother or my father. Pa used to let me stand on his feet while we

31

danced. I loved it. Music was a big part of our family life. All of us sang, and we loved harmonizing.

It was a happy time for me when I started first grade. I really liked my teacher, Sister Mary Pius. She sometimes left pastries inside my desk, which I called cupcakes. They must have been muffins leftover from her breakfast.

Tyler School in the 1940s

That year, Sister Mary Pius made me a costume so I could be in the school's annual show. How excited I was the day I went to the convent so she could measure me. Ma said I couldn't be in the show because we couldn't afford a costume. When I relayed that information to Sister Mary Pius, she suggested I ask my mother if she could make my costume so I could be in the show.

I went home and put on a pleading face, "Ma, I know you and Pa can't afford my costume, but Sister Mary Pius says they have material at school and she can make me one. Could I be in the show if she makes it? Please?"

Ma saw how important it was to me. "Yes, Joanie. You can be in that show if we don't have to buy material."

Now I was no longer going to be performing for my brothers and sisters, I was going to be on a real stage. I thought my debut was a smashing success.

My school years were fun for me. I loved having friends and learning all kinds of things. I also loved being in the shows we put on every year to raise money for the school. I would always look forward to being in the show. First, I was in specialties, then solos. My first specialty was "On the Boardwalk in Atlantic City." We wore long dresses and carried parasols as we paraded along the imaginary boardwalk where life was like walking in a dream.

I learned to tap-dance by watching the others at our weekly practices. In the next few years, the opportunity to dance the waltz-clog came my way. Those shows made me popular with the boys and the girls alike.

Since our grammar school included the ninth grade, I entered high school as a

The St. Xavier Academy building as it appears today, incorporated into the campus of Johnson and Wales University

sophomore. High school at St. Xavier Academy was different. My Spanish teacher told us that the word sophomore means "wise fool" in Greek. It served as a fair warning not to think we knew everything. Challenges would rear up before us, some unexpected. She was right.

My unforeseen challenge became meeting new people. The unfamiliar high school girls arranged their hair so beautifully and wore makeup. Although high school was more enjoyable once I got to know some of the girls, it was also troublesome. I couldn't socialize with them after school. I had to stay close to my own neighborhood because I worked after school. My family needed me to bring in an income. Money was always an issue for us.

My sister Patsy quit high school to work full time so I could stay in school. The tuition was too high to send both of us. This big sister of mine used the excuse that she quit high school because I liked school more than she did. Besides, she could go to work in the enameling shop where my father and brother worked.

I learned recently that Patsy had loved St. Xavier Academy the year she had spent there. Patsy has always been generous and giving. She is the only living sister I have today. When I talk to her on the phone these days, we laugh about silly things. She still lives in Rhode Island with her husband of sixty years in the same house they bought near the beginning of their marriage. I cherish all my early memories of her.

She is very sick these days and her loving husband is right there by her side.

Much happened during my three years at St. Xavier Academy. Those teen years opened my mind and my heart to so many beliefs, academics ... and boys.

A significant awakening took place in my typing room. Tacked on the bulletin board was the Prayer of St. Francis of Assisi. I stood mesmerized by the words that began, "Lord, make me an instrument of your peace..."

I remember thinking, *What a beautiful way to live!* To this day, the words of the Franciscan founder embody one of my favorite prayers, which guide my every step.

I had my fair share of dates. One was a sailor who brought flowers to my mother and cigars to my father and asked if he could have their permission to date me. I was surprised they said yes. We had fun, and I felt so free and happy. Then I found out his intentions were less than honorable, as we said in those days, and the relationship ended.

During these adventurous years. I was also interested in singing with a band. When I sang at my junior prom, the band leader gave me his card and said to come for an audition. He also made it clear that I had to bring my repertoire. I was very excited at this offer and diligently wrote the words to every song I knew on the white side of a shirt cardboard. I had taken this cardboard out of a freshly cleaned shirt one of my brothers hid in the piano bench. It seemed to be the perfect size for my repertoire. I sat at the kitchen table furiously writing and humming.

My mother walked by. "What in the world are you writing?"

I smiled delightedly. "It's my repertoire. The band leader who had played at the Junior Prom invited me for an audition to sing for him because he heard me and thought I was good."

She put her hands on her hips. "You rip that up right now and forget the notion of being a singer with a band."

I covered the cardboard with my hands. "Ma, I'm quite a good singer, and he really loved my singing." Her reaction was a shock to my system.

Shaking her head, my mother sat at the table

with me. "Joanie, you don't understand the ways of the world. Living that kind of life exposes a young girl to all kinds of danger—from men or from who-knows-what-else."

I hung my head. "Ma, this could be my big chance, and you're taking it away from me."

Ma leaned toward me and put a hand on my arm. "Joanie, I'm sure you sang well. I've heard you, and you have a lovely voice. But no daughter of mine will ever put herself into such a difficult and lonely life. That's final."

I launched my brand of teenage rebellion. "**** it, Ma. It's unfair for you to rob me of my dream. I may never have this chance again—to live my hope of becoming a star."

Later on, when I thought about it, relief flooded me. Ma had some good points. Besides, I had a much more powerful dream in my heart that had been with me before this band-singer possibility had come up.

Earlier that year I noticed how much I appreciated everything the nuns at St. Xavier taught me. I loved their values and how they helped so many people. They certainly showed great kindness and understanding to me and my family.

That year Sister Bernard had shared a recollection about the time she served as a missionary in Belize, British Honduras. I never wanted to go on missions to faraway places, but I loved the idea of becoming a nun and helping people. That dream continued to grow through my senior year.

I inquired what a person would do to enter the convent but never let on to others that I was considering the idea. My mother was quite surprised when I announced that I was going into the convent. Her comment was, "We'll have to see what your father has to say about that."

That wasn't a problem for me at all. Pa was my greatest supporter and had always encouraged me since my early childhood. Before our dinner ended that night, my mother asked me if I was going to tell Pa what I had told her. I hopped up from my seat at the table and went to where he was sitting. I threw my arms around his neck in an affectionate hug and made my declaration, "Pa, I'm going to be a nun."

He smiled. "You are? Are you sure you want to do this?"

"Oh, yes, Pa," I jiggled in my excitement. "I even know how to do it."

Tilting his head, he said, "What do you mean?" He seemed amused by my enthusiasm.

I was so happy to be able to tell him the whole story. "I called up Sister Mary Josephus and asked what steps to go through if you wanted to become a nun. She told me a whole bunch of things. You have to have a nun help you. You have to be sure you want to do this. You get some things ready to put in a trunk that could be shared with the other sisters, like blankets and sheets and pillow cases, stuff like that. Then you need some sturdy shoes and other things for yourself."

I rattled on and on about the things I had learned from my phone call to Sister Mary Josephus. I remembered I had laughed when Sister expressed curiosity about who needed this information. When I told her I asked for myself, she seemed happy. Now I hoped my father and mother would be happy too.

Then Pa stood up, put his hands on my shoulders and looked deeply into my eyes. In a somber voice, he asked, "Do you really want to do this, Joanie?"

My eager reassurance that I did made me seem so certain that Pa gave me his look of love and encouragement. What he said next would change my life for the next eighteen years. "If you do follow through on this dream of yours, just be a good nun, and pray for the rest of us."

Those words granting me permission began the preparation that would continue until the end of my senior year in high school and through the summer of 1954. I had tons of fun going shopping with Ma for things I would need to put in my trunk. One of the items was a pair of sensible shoes that looked like the ones my mother wore.

"Ma, look at me in these old lady shoes, and I'm only seventeen." I laughed and modeled the frumpy black footwear.

My mother didn't join in my laughter. "Joanie, you're joking around, but your decision about entering the convent has to be final. I'm not going to be putting out money and have you turn around and come back home just because you don't like the shoes."

I could see she was worried. "Ma, a pair of shoes would never get in the way of living my dream to be a nun."

Chapter 2—MY DREAM COME TRUE
ഇാര§ാര§ാര

My entrance day to training as a novice was September 8, 1954. I smoked my last cigarette on the way to the big brick building they called the Novitiate. The ride was glorious. We left the city of Providence to ascend into the lovely town of Cumberland, Rhode Island, less than fifteen miles away. The wooded scenery expressed how I felt—welcomed, embraced by nature itself. The landscape spoke to me of quiet, peaceful beauty.

As the car climbed the hill where I would make my new home, we passed a grotto. I discovered the Sisters came here to celebrate certain holy events or holy days. We reached the top of the hill and turned right. My breath was taken away by the fully grown, beautiful trees lining the road on both sides. My father stopped the car at the front entrance to my new home.

This experience foreshadowed a multitude of surprises revealing breathtaking beauty I would encounter during my six years in the Novitiate on Cumberland Hill. Having woods as my backyard was an entirely new way of experiencing nature's gorgeous display. The essence of the forest filled my heart. Every season I was gifted with natural beauty that never ceased to take my breath away. The transition from city girl to country girl suited me fine.

That day of my entrance into a new world of love and service is a cherished memory. Saying goodbye to my family seemed to be easier for me than for some of the other girls. I did an Irish jig in my "old lady" shoes and showed off my postulant dress and veil. My family rejoiced with me at my commitment to God.

On the other hand, I noticed some tearful families struggling with saying goodbye. Some of the girls wept while we climbed the stairs to our dormitory, but I was surprised because my heart sang with joy. Being at the novitiate fulfilled my dream. I had come home.

Community living was an easy adjustment after growing up in a large family. Sharing space and accepting assignments to manage our dormitory was normal for me. I took these responsibilities in stride and happily shared the workload.

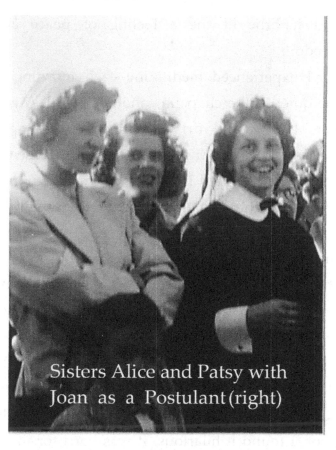

Sisters Alice and Patsy with Joan as a Postulant (right)

Arriving on time was another matter. In Tyler School, the administration and teachers called us "the late McDermotts." In the convent, when late, I had to bow to the Superior before I could take my seat at our chapel functions. In spite of this, the regimentation suited me. I had learned at home that order is Heaven's first law, and it brought me a feeling of peace and freedom.

I experienced meditating each morning in the quiet of the chapel as another priceless gift. The bird song drifted through the open windows in the silence of the dawn. Because the chapel was divided into sides, the sisters on the right side would chant the first line of the Psalm and the next line was chanted by the sisters on the left side. Chanting on alternating sides of the chapel created a meditative state of being and brought me to a happy place in my heart each morning.

I was very late one morning, gliding into the chapel with my untied corset strings trailing behind me. When I discovered the strings on the floor, I found it hilarious. It was hard for me to muffle my laughter, and even harder to get into a state of meditation. I managed to get through the psalms, then had to leave the chapel to fix the problem. I still didn't know why I had to wear a corset, as slim as I was. The nuns said it was "good for back support." Of course, I didn't argue.

I loved all the activities in the novitiate and never grew tired of any of them. Everything seemed so new and fresh and worthwhile. The woods in the back of the property fascinated me. I explored them at every opportunity.

A memorable transformative experience occurred one winter. We had snow the night before, and I went walking in it. My footsteps crunched in the white stuff down the familiar paths through the silent woods. The pristine odor of new-fallen snow clung in my nostrils. Wet snow weighed heavily on the branches of the trees.

I stopped dead in my tracks in awe of the scene before me. The pure white snow had created a sparkling winter dreamworld.

I had the impulse to make angels in the

snow. I fell on my back to make the arm movements that would create the wings and scissored my legs to make the angel's skirt. The silent peace and stillness of God's world descended on me as I played in the snow. For a city girl, this was a little bit of heavenly bliss.

The woods were also a place to escape from the novice who made it her job to keep us postulants in check. My friend and I plotted to discover if we still liked to smoke. We hatched a plan—She would find the cigarettes, and I would steal the matches. Then we would escape into the woods to have a smoke.

She saw cigarettes on the front seat of the grounds keeper's car. He usually left his car window open so she easily grabbed them in one swift movement. We headed to the chapel to abscond with the matches from the shrine in the back. These were for visitors who came to pray and light a candle.

No sooner did I have the matches in my hand when a visitor came in. I dropped the box of matches while laughing at our ridiculous scheme. I knelt and grabbed my handkerchief from my pocket, using it to cover my face, pretending I was crying. My shoulders shook with laughter, but I hoped my fake crying would make her think I was praying over some tragedy.

After the visitor left, I scooped up the matches, and we rushed into the woods. When we were deep enough into the trees to be hidden, we lit up and puffed away on a cigarette. That busybody novice called our names from the edge of the forest. She was on to us. It was time to go back to the compound.

We had to cut our little escapade short, but we reeked of smoke. On the way back we whispered to each other that we didn't like smoking any more—mission accomplished. Although we stank of smoke, no one mentioned the smell or even seemed to notice us.

After that, my conscience bothered me so I told the priest in confession. I wonder if he stifled his laughter while I shared what I thought was such sinful behavior.

I shared my confession. "Bless me Father, for I have sinned. My friend and I stole some cigarettes from the front seat of the grounds-keeper's car. Then I stole some matches from the shrine of Our Lady of Perpetual Help. After that we went to hide in the woods to smoke. We just wanted to see if we still liked smoking." He asked me what I had learned from this.

"Well," I said, "we both decided we didn't like smoking anymore."

He asked me if I was sorry for what I had done. When I assured him that I was, he told me to say some prayers and recite my Act of Contrition. Then he gave me absolution and told me to go in peace.

It all seemed so silly when I thought about it, but then again, stealing is a sin. The seventh commandment tells us, "Thou shalt not steal."

That first year of my postulancy was a year of adjustment to so many inner and outer changes. I was quite adaptable and very grateful for everything I learned and lived through. I felt in my heart that the convent was the right place for me.

Receiving my veil felt like getting a trophy or an award. I was so excited to know this was the real thing. When my beautiful hair was shaved, I saw no reason to cry over losing it, because I gained the veil of an authentic nun to wear on my head.

Tonsure, the act of shaving the head as a sign of religious devotion, seemed much harder for others. When we all paraded into the chapel wearing our white veils, hands folded in prayer position, our families whispered loving expressions of awe. The beautiful hymn our choir sang enraptured me. I felt elated … and complete.

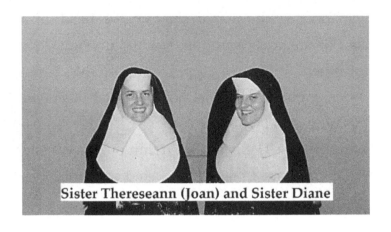

Sister Thereseann (Joan) and Sister Diane

Chapter 4—SPIRITUAL AND EMOTIONAL GROWTH

ഇ൬ഇ൬ഇ൬

The personal growth I would undergo in this all-encompassing life as a nun-in-the-making, had only begun. This formative period came with many surprises that were not always pleasant.

I grew more aware that four of the twenty-two novices didn't accept me. Their demeaning remarks and criticisms were a shock to my happy-go-lucky system. Their cruel treatment made no sense to me. In the twenty-first century, we would call these girls "bullies." I thought we had all come to the convent to express love and kindness for God and for one another. This first big challenge began a downward spiral of confusion and darkness that sent me into a battle within my heart and soul and disrupted my usual feelings of joy and well-being.

One of my fellow novices, Sister Diane, became my best friend. What a blessing it was to have such a great ally who had my best interests at heart. She was popular with many of the girls, and protected me from some of the mean things they said about me.

I wasn't good at honoring or even naming my feelings, never mind expressing them, and I had a hard time talking about the situation to Diane. I did tell her that they upset me with their taunts. Without realizing it, I plunged into grieving the death of my dream of what being a nun was like. The profound disappointment triggered my first episode of depression.

I did what I knew how to do best and hid my hurt feelings. Being able to turn to my best friend provided a buffer that gave me some relief. This group of girls who had been criticizing and laughing at me called me a "goody two-shoes" and a "phony." I felt powerless and afraid of them. They came off as a gang, all coming from the same town and all projecting the same superior attitude.

Sister Diane wasn't afraid--she saw some-thing in them I couldn't see. I used the shield of her friendship as my protection against their hurtful attacks. If Diane didn't think I was a worthless phony, I must not be. This new way of looking at myself gave me the strength to ignore them and focus on what I was doing that gave me joy.

When I no longer reacted to their taunts, the gang of girls seemed to lose interest in laughing at me. Whether that was because they saw that Diane, whom they liked, was my friend, or because I no longer reacted to what they were saying, I'll never know.

Whatever it was, I felt the relief of having shared my feelings with Diane. I was to learn this lesson several times in my life. We are as sick as the secrets we hold. They eat at us inside. Sharing with someone we trust is a helpful way to expose the sickening feelings poisoning our souls.

In the end, most of the mean girls left the convent before our profession of final vows. I don't know if it was because the nuns asked them to leave, or if the girls chose to leave

Everyday living resumed, and I experienced a sense of growth through all my changes. A short time later, another unexpected blanket of darkness fell over me, and I crashed hard. The feelings of blackness were so foreign and confusing to me that I began to question my sanity.

This serious episode of depression manifested as feelings of heaviness in my body and limbs and lethargy that kept me from getting going. Since I didn't have words to describe it, I couldn't talk to anybody about it. Not being able to share magnified my feelings of loneliness, isolation, and fear. All I could do was tough it out and pray more than usual.

As I searched for reasons for my feelings, the personal responsibility of living a life that seemed so large and demanding loomed before me. Perhaps the depression was triggered by feeling ostracized by the "mean postulants." Grieving is inevitable in a life of unexpected changes. I learned more about grief and depression in this uncharted area of convent living.

My standard method of coping since childhood was to keep moving on. For a second time, the darkness lifted, and I was able to live my everyday life with more focus. In those days,

I hadn't found words for my deepest feelings. All I knew was the pain inside. I had so much to learn about my emotional life on the road to becoming a mature woman.

As I reflect on these two early instances in my newly embraced sisterhood, it has become clear to me that awareness of self and the motivation of others always gives me a chance at better choices. Years passed before I became clear about that fact. As the young woman who had just entered her twenties with a history of "just getting on with her life," my personal evolution was at the mercy of the push and pull in my life. I was hardly making any choices at all.

My love of nature grew. On the East Coast, Mother Nature was at her best all the seasons of the year. I graciously received many wonderful gifts from God's creative hands; he filled my hungry heart. What a joy to be able to skate my way across the frozen pond, singing in the winter. When spring arrived, the flowers popped up, their lovely heads enthralling me with fresh life showing the wonders of creation.

The birds sang outside the chapel windows during meditation. They filled my soul with songs of praise and gratitude. Summer's gift of nature found me lying on a big flat rock in the middle of a garden. I lay there resting, kissed by the sun that I loved so, as it filled me with warmth. My autumn walk to the grotto surrounded me with leaves showing their best breathtaking fall colors. Cumberland Hill and all its magnificence blessed me and wrapped me in a mantle of love and Divine mystery.

The splendor of my surroundings intertwined with growing pains as each year brought me closer to my final profession. Each learning opportunity fine-tuned my insight into why I was there in the first place. Theology classes and interactions with teachers carried me to my graduation with a bachelor's from the Mercy College of Education in my twenties.

We had a small ceremony, not a grand one like graduates from other colleges. We didn't wear caps and gowns, nor did we have to find a job. We were prepared to become teachers in schools already established by the Order of the

Sisters of Mercy.

Becoming a Religious Sister of Mercy integrated the physical, intellectual, and spiritual elements of living. I rejoiced in the time I spent becoming familiar with the skills that would allow me

Joan with Statue of Catherine McAuley in Dublin, Ireland

to lead a purposeful life of integrity and compassionate service. Our Irish Foundress, Mother Catherine McAuley, had a deep devotion to the Mercy of God. All of our work was to bring that spirit into all our compassionate works of mercy in the service of God and of all humankind.

Religious sisters ventured into the community and worked with people in a life of service. Religious Sisters of Mercy helped the poor, taught in schools founded by our order, or provided healthcare in our hospitals. We lived under vows the same as monastic sisters did.

After six years of study, meditation, and prayer, we took our final vows. The years spent in formation and examination of whether or not I truly wanted to commit to a lifetime of serving the poor, the sick and the uneducated ended, and I professed my vows as Sister Mary Thereseann, RSM. I knew in my mind and heart I was in the right place and gladly became a Religious Sister of Mercy. My next exciting move was to my first mission, which is what we called our assignments.

I couldn't have been more pleased with my mission in North Providence, which was to teach a large class of second-grade boys and girls at St. Ann's. The school was similar to the one where I started first grade. The classroom was filled to the brim with seven- and eight-year-olds.

I loved teaching. One of the fun things I taught was music, where the students learned songs, some of which my father had written. When anyone came to visit our classroom, we would entertain them with a song. My second graders would sing their little hearts out using all the hand gestures I taught them to go with the words. I proudly showed off the talents of my class.

I continued teaching second grade the next year in that same school, and on my next mission, I became a third-grade teacher. I liked this grade even better. Each year the administration of the Sisters of Mercy assigned me to another school, where I taught a different grade. I liked fifth grade the best.

In one of the schools, I taught a group of seventh graders to sing in harmony. My little choral group entered a competition, but I noticed that there were other schools with much more polished singing groups. It was embarrassing for me, and I learned more about what the standards in other schools were like. One of my brothers came to watch, and his brotherly criticism was generous. I ate a lot of humble pie that day.

Nevertheless, the principal where I led the choral group thought I had musical talent. She recommended that the sisterhood send me to Marywood College in Pennsylvania where I studied elementary school music for two summers. Unfortunately, when I received my next teaching assignment, my music studies ended. I had enjoyed them a great deal, and thought back to how I loved singing in childhood.

Moving so often required more growth on my part than staying at the same school for years would have. I discovered then what I have come to believe now—every move was a loss that compelled me to look at life in a new way. Each new school brought different personalities, different rules and regulations, and pleasant and not-so-pleasant surprises.

Chapter 5—SUMMERS IN ALLEGANY

ຂດເຂດເຂດ

One of the surprises was an offer to attend St. Bonaventure University summer classes in upstate New York to work toward a Master of Arts in theology. The Franciscan Order founded the university in 1858 as St. Bonaventure's College, and it was granted university status in 1950.

Six summers of study for my master's degree started in the mid-1960s. Traveling to upstate New York offered me a new adventure. Allegany, New York in the Allegheny mountains near the Pennsylvania border lay almost five hundred miles from my home in Rhode Island. This was only the second time I left my home state.

Exposure to a different kind of atmosphere in this magical place filled me with a joy that put a bounce in my steps as I walked through the campus grounds. Everyone I met exuded friendliness and greeted people they passed with a smile and pleasant "hello." I had been apprehensive about traveling so far, but the students and faculty on the campus made me feel so comfortable that I reveled in a new-found sense of freedom.

I explored the entire grounds; my favorite place to visit daily was the elegant chapel. Outside, a statue of St. Francis of Assisi kneels, looking up at the bell tower of the chapel. Inside, the expansive stained-glass windows, manufactured in Paris, depict St. Bonaventure's life story.

Near the chapel lay a stand of forested land. In the center of all that greenery, I discovered the campus beekeeper, who fascinated me with his protective regalia. He went out among the trees to work with the bees every day. After a while, he allowed me to sit on a bench nearby and watch him and the bees perform their interplay. The buzzing creatures had a close relationship with this gentle beekeeper. Each knew what their particular job was, and they performed their tasks with synergy, producing results that were greater than the energy contributed by either. I felt privileged to sit quietly and behold this graceful dance choreographed by none other than the Creator. The spiritual aspect of the experience stirred my heart and reaffirmed my love of the beauty of nature.

***

One day, a group of us graduate student nuns hiked up one of the nearby mountains — another first for me. As we relaxed on the mountain top, I gazed at the picturesque view of a farm below. Thinking it reminded me of a photo in a magazine, I went into a meditative state and rejoiced there for a while. As I drifted in my own mind, studies seemed of secondary importance to this experiential education.

The six glorious summers I could enjoy these many incredible gifts expanded my heart in the spirit of freedom and wonder. My St. Bonaventure campus life proved to be a priceless memory of love and learning in a myriad of ways.

I never understood why the nuns who studied with me were so anxious about their tests and classes. I was having the time of my life. Of course, my dear friend Sister Joan C. shared her well-taken notes with me and helped me prepare for exams.

I just loved St. Bonaventure's. The people on campus were like a friendly family. I have so many happy memories during these Bonaventure days. I met Mike at St. Bonaventure University, and he would end up playing a very important role in my life. Mike was taking make-up courses in history at the University, although he lived in New Haven, Connecticut.

Father Gabe, a Franciscan priest, studied with us. He and I started a campus ministry group, where he played his guitar. We mixed well with the college kids.

Father Gabe celebrated Mass in one of the dorm rooms. It didn't matter what the students' religion was, or if they had any religion at all. Father would have what he called the "bread and wine of friendship" so they could participate in our liturgy, although the Catholics partook of consecrated bread and wine.

Many students participated in the Mass. After the Scripture readings, everyone had a chance to share what portions had spoken to their hearts as they listened. We sang to Father's guitar accompaniment. The young people filled the room and spilled out into the hall as our group continued to grow. As the summers went by, a few times we went with them to a restaurant that had a bar. I was so struck by their childlike joy as we did the Hokey Pokey and other group dances.

I never noticed any of them leaving the group to drink at the bar. The first few summers I didn't want to drink when we went out with them. That changed as time went on.

By the sixth summer when I received my Master of Arts in theology, I was no longer Sister Mary Thereseann, In 1970, I became Joan McDermott.

Chapter 6—LESSONS IN GRACE

ഇരുജ്ജ ഇരുജ്ജ ഇരുജ്ജ

Back in Rhode Island, I moved from school to school as my teaching days continued. When I moved to East Greenwich, I fell in love with the little town. My walks took me to a pleasant street called Love Lane. The stately homes and gardens carried me into a fantasy land. One of my favorite homes was bordered by a hand-laid rock wall. I often saw a charming woman who puttered in her garden as I walked by. She seemed friendly, so I engaged her in conversation. What a nice surprise for me to discover her love of God and connection with the church. She shared with me that she was undergoing cancer treatment. Her warmth and positive, loving ways inspired me. When I left her, my heart was full of love.

The Superior of the convent saw me return from my walk one day. "Sister Mary Therese-ann, have you completed your chores?"

I nodded. "Yes, Sister. I've been on a walk to Love Lane, where there is a forested area with beautiful homes and lovely gardens. I had a conversation with a woman who lives there about her love of the Lord. She is afflicted with cancer, and is being treated for it, but her sunny disposition hasn't dimmed at all. She doesn't question God's will for her. I found our conversation so uplifting." I smiled, expecting her to share my joy.

Instead, Sister scowled. "You are not supposed to go out for walks without my permission. What are you thinking, wandering all over creation alone?"

This Sister struggled with being a Superior, and the other sisters didn't like her. Instead of sulking and huffing off, I chose to apologize and explain I wasn't aware of that rule. I hoped to ease her stress and also improve my relationship with her. When I moved to East Greenwich, I had chosen her as the person I most wanted to be kind to. I could appreciate how difficult her job was, given the factors she was up against.

My attitude proved effective for both of us. When I received my new teaching assignment the next year, she wrote me a note and expressed her gratitude for my kindness. That made me happy.

I didn't suspect my next teaching assignment would be my last for a while. It was quite an extraordinary year. Bay View Academy was different from all the other places where I had lived. It consisted of two buildings. The larger building housed the chapel, senior sisters who needed care, and an extension to the high school and gym. The other building housed dormitories for the boarders and a few elementary grade classrooms. I lived on the side with the boarders, and I was back to teaching second grade in the small elementary school situated in the same building.

So much went on in this huge complex. The walkway between the chapel and the sleeping quarters had no cover to protect us from the rain or snow, and we walked to it every day. I liked visiting the elderly nuns in that building.

When I discovered an indoor walkway to get into the high school gym, I used the gym for jogging whenever I had the time, provided the students weren't there. Physical movement satisfied the part of me that loved to exercise. My father was an athlete, and as a young girl I had been drawn into reading his exercise books.

The Second Vatican Council, from 1962 to 1965, updated many practices of the Roman Catholic Church, including congregation-friendlier Mass, more open relations with other denominations, and more relaxed rules for clergy. Secular clothes became an option in place of our habits. By the end of 1968, The Sisters of Mercy made changes in their practices.

Another major change was the opportunity to choose where we would like to serve rather than being assigned. We could use our individual God-given talents to enhance our service to others. I chose secular clothes and a new world of child-care work at St. Aloysius Home. The home had been an orphanage in the past, but it had become a place for children from broken homes whose families couldn't care for them.

I was granted my choice of what change in work I wanted to make and must admit that what I chose turned out to be extremely challenging. We received excellent training from a psychologist who taught me how to work with the girls assigned to me. My thirteen charges were the only girls in the home, and they were wild, to say the least. The most important thing I learned was that despite making all the mistakes

The Ice Test: Sister Thereseann takes her friends, Dottie and Terry, across new skating rink at the St. Aloysius Home in Greenville. The trio was trying out the ice after ceremonies Saturday afternoon during which the half-acre rink was dedicated. Sister Thereseann works at the children's home.
—Journal-Bulletin Photo

in the world, if I sincerely loved these girls, they would know that, and no serious harm would be done.

I did love them, and I always believed that love never fails. My creativity in thinking of things to do with them surprised me, and surrogate parenting came naturally to me. We did so many fun things together, like holding group meetings where they could create their own rules.

This worked and gave them a sense of empowerment. It brought order into the chaotic world of their lives. Dormitory life wasn't easy for them.

Since I'd never learned to drive, I signed up for driving lessons so I could use the home's van to take my girls shopping. At first, I ferried a few girls at a time to buy some new clothes. Driving in the van with them gave me a chance to get to know them outside of their St. Aloysius Home surroundings. While keeping within our budget, I also purchased some colorful bedspreads and drapes to brighten their environment.

I discovered some bureaus stored in the basement of St. Aloysius. The girls had the ugliest furniture in their rooms, and these old bureaus were nicer than what they had. After receiving permission from the administrator, I called some of my friends to help the girls antique their bureaus. Each girl had a different woman helping her paint her dresser. The girls loved all of the new activities I brought into their lives and engaged in fewer shenanigans and high jinks than when I first arrived.

In the middle of my second year there, the local Catholic administration of Providence replaced the administrator and group director of the Home. Both of these women were my friends and were instrumental in my choice to become a childcare worker. The administrator left to pursue an opportunity in psychiatric nursing, a profession she had been trained for. She answered the call to render service using her personal gifts and skills.

The group director became ill and was in need of the kind of help beyond what the Sisters could provide. She left the order, returning home so her family could care for her.

I experienced loss during my years at the home. My friends in the administration left, and their replacements didn't think highly of me.

They told me in a disdainful manner that I spent too much time away from my group of girls. They weren't happy when I sometimes returned late from my time off. I felt their criticisms were not only unfair, but untrue, and they made me angry and resentful. I had worked very hard with the girls, but my superiors never commented on that. I felt unappreciated, lost, and lonely.

The horrors of rape reared up during those two years at St. Aloysius Home. I was too afraid to think about it or talk about it at the time. My driving instructor had raped me.

I was frightened and in shock, but moreover, I was filled with shame and self-loathing. I never told anyone about it, carrying the secret in the depths of my broken spirit. Feelings of profound guilt and confusion stopped me from sharing what happened. I could never tell any of this to the people who shared my home. I was too hurt, overwhelmed, and exhausted from managing their disrespect. I deeply resented the new administrator, who only criticized me and never pointed out the good I did.

I used the same coping strategy I had used

in the past and hid my feelings. The external pressure the new administrators placed on me to live up to their expectations, and the internal pressure of the rape took their toll on me emotionally.

Feelings of rage began to manifest. I hadn't used bad language since I was a teen, but curse words re-emerged from my lips. I let go with irritable behaviors that took my girls by surprise. What shook me was how aggravated I acted with the girls when they slipped into their own acting out from depressive behaviors that originated from being mistreated by their families. They didn't deserve to take the brunt of my emotional breakdown.

Fighting to keep all that inside ate away at my body, mind, and spirit. My life was falling apart, making my need for quiet reflection increasingly important. I gave up trying to manage the unmanageable. Loss of control had taken its toll in every area of my life. The strain caught up with me at the end of that year, and I asked if I could move to our House of Prayer. I had to get back to the garden.

The House of Prayer had formerly been the Provincialate of the northeastern Province. The governing board of sisters for that region operated out of that "house on the hill" in Cumberland, Rhode Island. When they changed the location of their headquarters, the house was converted into a Retreat House. People came there when they needed some time to renew their lives with prayer in the peaceful surroundings of this sacred place.

The House of Prayer sat on the top of Cumberland Hill, down the road from the Novitiate. Nearby was the lake where we used to ice skate when I was a novice. To reach the lake, we took a path through peaceful woods. That particular environment was the best place for me to return to—I started and ended my life as a nun there. How fortunate for me that the Sisters of Mercy converted it to a House of Prayer about the time all the updates to the Church occurred.

I had made the best decision of my life and was so grateful I had been given permission to move there. The retreatants were people that came to us for a variety of reasons. My friend, "Janice the Junkie," whom some of us had befriended back in Providence, came to get off drugs. Couples came to renew their relationships, and groups came to have a week of retreat. We welcomed anyone who needed a place like ours, and the best part was that visitors weren't charged a fee, but donated what they felt the experience was worth to them, or what they could afford.

I've had a dream for a few years now to establish a retreat house like that. Anything is possible with God—who knows? It seems outlandish to have such a dream in my financial state right now, but a dream is a dream, and that is mine.

The Sisters, and at that time I was one of them, prepared their meals, set up their rooms and gave whatever service was needed. We cooked and cleaned and let those in retreat choose how they wanted to use their time.

Thankfully, the Sisters of Mercy administration granted me permission to live there. I worked out the details about how to leave my beloved girls to whom I had committed myself.

It was a most difficult decision that plagued me with guilt feelings for abandoning them. In addition, I still struggled with the guilt and shame surrounding the rape. But leaving the St. Aloysius Home was the best decision for me because the Administrator hit me almost every day with new unreasonable demands and criticisms that sent me deeper into depression.

Becoming part of our House of Prayer staff turned out to be the door leading to the healing of my troubled heart. When I arrived, I was broken and exhausted. Being a surrogate mother of thirteen girls required oceans of energy, both physical and emotional. Piling on the heavy load of two friends moving away, constant criticism, and the weight of being raped and not talking about it just about did me in.

Melodie Beatty, in her book, *The Language of Letting Go: Daily Meditations for Codependents*, called denial a friend who was also an enemy. I can see now how I was using denial as a friend that got me through much of this period. I bought myself a little time and was graced with the space to get the help I needed.

Most of my time while living at the Retreat House was spent as a fifth-grade teacher in our Mercymount Country Day School that was not quite a mile down the road. Eleven boys and eleven girls were in my fifth-grade class. It was like heaven to me. It seemed like a perfect number of children, and teaching them was a joy. I remember the day my students and I walked up the hill to the Retreat House. They thought it was so beautiful. We visited the chapel and said a prayer, and I showed them around the grounds. It was special to me and to them.

My teaching was also a way of bringing in money to keep up with some of the Retreat House expenses. We offered the retreats on a donation basis, if the retreatants could afford one. Somehow, the Retreat House always had enough money to pay the bills.

The chaplain there had been given a leave of absence from his monastery to learn about the Charismatic Renewal that was happening in the Church. Catholics had begun to join with our Protestant brothers and sisters in prayer meetings. I had been participating in these prayer meetings for some time by then. They suited me fine, and I loved the wonderful experience of expressing prayer with spontaneous song and sharing Bible readings.

Our chaplain became my spiritual advisor. It was so helpful to have a humble, holy monk to talk to. He had a pure, receptive heart, and my healing began from being able to talk with him about all that was troubling me. One of the things I brought up often was why I didn't feel like serving the people anymore. It was shocking to me. All my life I had a great desire to love and help others, even as a child. These new and self-absorbed feelings filled me with shame and guilt.

One day when I engaged in what I called my "true confessions," Father made the observation that I had been saying the same things again and again for the last three months. He alluded to the possibility that maybe I needed to do something else with my life. I began to tremble from anxiety. He couldn't possibly be saying I should leave the convent. That never entered my thoughts. Giving up my life as a nun didn't make sense to me. I couldn't be part of the external world. I never questioned my commitment to God.

His next words were, "I'm not telling you to leave nor am I telling you to stay, but I would like to make a suggestion. Sit with your Bible in a quiet place and open your mind and heart to invite enlightenment. Don't be surprised at what the Holy Spirit may blow in."

His words stunned me, but because I was a prayerful and devout person, I did as Father suggested. I sat in the quiet of my room with a glass of wine in my hand and my Bible in my lap. I waited to get some kind of inspiration. Nothing happened!

I looked up at God and said, "You're not telling me anything, so this is what I'm going to do. I'll leave the convent because no one seems to know what's wrong with me, and you'll take care of me."

To be sure that I was on the right track I opened the Bible and just so happened to turn to Zephaniah. I looked at God and said, "The Old

Testament? Couldn't you at least give me a gospel reading?"

What a surprise I had when I read and interpreted Zephaniah 3. God said to me what he said to his people who had lost their way. He gave me three promises if I changed my ways. God would remove my shame, renew me in His love, and set me as a light for others. "Wow, good deal God" I said as I closed the Bible.

I began making plans as to how I would be released from my vows, find a job, and figure out where to live. It would take me the rest of the year to accomplish this, and I could only do it with God's grace and love. I had no idea of the full ramifications of this major change God led me to make.

I felt deeply committed to saying personal, loving goodbyes to the elderly nuns that had shown so much affection for me. They were very dear to my heart and I visited each one to let her know I was leaving. It was difficult because they had looked at me—a young nun—as the hope of the community. They were surprised and saddened by my decision, but wanted the very best for me and assured me of their prayers. Their sincere wishes for me were comforting and made my departure a bit easier.

I looked for a teaching job and housing that would be close to where I worked. I made a few phone calls and was able to find a teaching position in a parochial school. It was situated near the home of a friend of Mike's from St. Bonaventure University. He and his wife were willing to let me live with them until I was on my feet and could afford an apartment of my own.

Telling my mother and father I was leaving the convent was the most difficult part. They'd planned a trip to California and I didn't want to tell them before they left. I was afraid they'd cancel their trip, so I waited until they were safely there and being nicely spoiled by my brother and his big family. I'm glad I did, even though my brother wasn't. He told me later that my mother couldn't stop crying. I think she believed my role as a nun would save the family and took my departure very hard. I asked Bishop Reilly, a beloved friend of many years, to talk with her. My plan was to visit her after I had settled into my new life "in the world."

A nun came to visit the Retreat House just at the time I left. She held a position in our Provincialate and was very knowledgeable regarding the procedure to be released from vows. I so appreciated all the loving help she gave me in that process. I was also very happy that all my sister friends were supportive. They made it known that I would always be warmly received if I visited. It has been so until this day, and I cherish each and every priceless memory of those eighteen years of consecrated life.

Chapter 7—A WOMAN OF THE WORLD

I finished out the school year, and made arrangements for someone to pick me up from Cumberland Hill at the Retreat House. The plan was to set up my classroom, then move into the home of Mike's friend.

I called the priest who told me about the teaching position and asked how soon I would be able to set up my classroom. He informed me the school had given that position to a nun. A nun's salary would be less than a secular teacher's pay. It was a moment of painful clarity that I was now a woman of the world and no longer protected by my nun's habit. I had to make it on my own.

With that awareness came another—I would need to find a cheaper place to live. Mike's sister told me one of her friends would let me stay with her while I looked for a job. We went to check it out. It turned out to be quite an eye opener. Cats jumped in and out of the broken screens on her windows, the place wasn't clean, and the house reeked with the smell of pot. I heard Mike and his sister's boyfriend whispering to each other, "She can't live here."

Mike's sister had a boyfriend who had just rented an apartment in New Haven. Their happy conclusion was that I could live with him. The small flat featured a bedroom on the other side of the kitchen, giving it some privacy. It seemed the perfect solution. Since I was standing there with a suitcase in one hand and a guitar in the other, basically homeless, all my friends agreed it would be the best option.

So, there I lived, strumming the guitar and singing "There's a New World Somewhere." Mike and his sister came by every day, and we all got along as great friends.

I continued making calls to find a new job. Working on campus in a ministry position would suit me best. After many hours on the phone, I found a priest who wanted to hire a woman co-chaplain part time. I went for an interview with Father Devore and got the job. It was in Bridgeport, Connecticut. The neighborhood had been deteriorating but the University of Bridgeport campus was lovely, although architecturally dated. I would be serving in the Newman Center, an organization for the Catholic students living on campus. Bridgeport was located two hours from Providence where my family lived and only twenty-five minutes from New Haven, where Mike and my other friends lived.

The day Father Devore introduced me to the students, he proclaimed I came from Rhode Island and asked them to welcome me as their new woman chaplain. He also added that I had a second job on campus and needed a place to live. A couple of the students told us about a nice place nearby that showed a "For Rent" sign in the window.

With that, Father and I hopped in his car and drove the short distance to investigate. The Italian woman who opened the door was so pleased to see the priest that she not only let me rent the apartment, but took me to her basement and showed me her laundry room with all the necessary supplies. She also told me I could use her vacuum cleaner, as long as I put the vacuum back when I finished with it. When she heard I didn't have a television set she brought one from her apartment and placed it in the corner of my living/dining room area. She was not only overjoyed to see the priest, but I believe she was happy to have a woman renter who wouldn't be fixing a motorcycle in the apartment like the previous tenants. It was a banner day for me too, finding two jobs and an apartment, and I felt safe with her caring ways.

The sweetness of the apartment, which was fully furnished, became such a comfort to me. It was small and set up so perfectly. A new friend from the university made beautiful drapes for me. She told me they would afford me the privacy I needed. Everything had worked out, and I felt blessed with so much kindness. I knew God was taking good care of me, as I had asked.

I was filled with gratitude. Knowing I was safe and cared for was balm to my body and soul. Being thankful brought me new life and a joy that energized me to move with confidence toward the life that was before me. There was a bounce to my step and I allowed myself to be open to all the new experiences coming my way.

The clearing space was quickly filled with so much grace, and became another example of finding new life after loss.

My life became very busy in Bridgeport. I worked in the office of the Director of Plant Engineering during the day. My job was to answer the phone and do a little filing. My boss treated me like I was his own daughter, and sometimes we just talked. He shared with me stories about his out-of-town trips, and I shared my life as a nun. He was fascinated and curious, and I was touched by his fatherly affection.

Chapter 8—EXPOSURE OF THE LIE

୨୦୯୫୨୦୯୫୨୦୯୫

Next to the building where I worked in Plant Engineering was the Newman Center where the students could hang out. When I wasn't working in the office, I ministered to these people as their chaplain.

A few offered to educate me about the world of drugs, and I found their information helpful, since some of the people who came to us used drugs. One weekly program I held in the early evening was called "Wine and Words." The attendees would read a piece of writing that they liked to the group. Some read a poem, a paragraph from a story, a reading from the Bible, or any other passage. After they shared why they chose it, each of us would comment on how the reading had affected us. Wine was available, and the atmosphere relaxed. I refilled my own glass more than once or twice, discreetly at first so the others wouldn't notice.

I didn't like the dishonest feeling I got from sneaking the extra wine. What I didn't admit to myself was that I had developed a love for the effects a little wine had on me. This started when I was at the House of Prayer; I would come back from teaching school and have a nip of wine. After drinking, I took a nap that refreshed me enough to continue to work into the evening, providing service to the people who were in Retreat. I used to tell the other Sisters how a "nip and a nap" were so helpful to me. Little did I know I was a budding alcoholic.

As I look back over these words I've written, it occurs to me how I used denial in my early days of drinking. No one wants to admit they have a problem with alcohol, so they protect themselves from that knowledge with the language they use to talk about their alcohol use. My three to four glasses of wine were "a little wine" or a "nip." I considered drinking "enjoyable" and "helpful." The negative effects of alcohol on my life didn't start until later, but I maintained my denial ...

Over the course of the year I spent as co-chaplain at the Newman Center, my drinking accelerated. On the way home from work, I would pick up a bottle of wine or vodka so I could have a drink before bed. I soon discovered that wine was fine, but liquor was quicker. I also got drunk when my friend Mike would pick me up for his basketball games. After the games, Mike's team and I would go to the bar to discuss the plays that occurred during the game. Since I wasn't really interested in their discussions, I would leave them sitting at the table, step up to the bar, and drink my martinis there.

Alcoholism, as you may know, is a progressive disease. My problem was that I knew nothing about alcoholism and was in deep denial about what I was doing. The natural course of alcoholism is to drink more and more and cause more significant and serious problems for oneself and the people in one's life.

Later on, I would learn that one characteristic of the alcoholic is to blame other people for the trouble that is brought about by their own excessive drinking. I would yell at Mike because he took me to those bars. Once when I was drunk after coming home from the bar, I slipped on the ice and banged my head, causing a concussion. Of course, I blamed it all on Mike. I was not getting drunk every day, so I never considered the idea that I was on the road to alcoholism. It was early in the game, and my life was busy and often fun and fulfilling. Because the problems were balanced by the good things, denial and deception about my drinking worked.

More and more, drinking seemed to rule over my life. My thinking became skewed, but I was unaware of the reality of this developing problem.

I remember a man who came to the Newman Center to just hang out. He seemed friendly, but I never thought much of it. One night he took me to dinner. Afterward, he tried to get me to kiss him, which made me uncomfortable, so I let him know I wasn't interested in a relationship with him. After dinner he took me to the Newman Center and walked me inside. The college kids who were there couldn't wait to tell me about the movie on television. Mary Tyler Moore starred as a nun who left the convent. I was interested in how that might be portrayed, but I didn't want to use their television because some of them might want to watch something else. I said I would go home to watch it.

My dinner date offered to take me home. On the way, he expressed a desire to see the movie too. I said okay, although I was surprised that he would be interested in a movie about an ex-nun.

I was right. He wasn't interested in the movie about an ex-nun. He had other ideas about the ex-nun he was with. Before the movie was half-over, he raped me. It was shocking and traumatic. I didn't see it coming.

My whole body shut down, and I froze, unable to fight him off. I had no voice to scream and holler. I had no strength to kick him out of the apartment. I had no ability to fight him off. I tried to push him away, but I felt like a child who was powerless over his assault. I became silent and terrified, and let him do what he was doing. My body was numb—it was as if I wasn't in my body, and had retreated to a place of safety, watching it happen from outside myself.

When it was all over, he departed without saying a word. I was left trembling, tearful, and dissociated. The next morning, I was filled with shame, confusion, and deep remorse. I believed I should have stopped him, should have fought him off, should have done something … anything, despite my feelings of utter powerlessness the night before.

When he telephoned me at work, my body shook with fear. His voice took on a threatening tone. "Don't call that rape," he would say.

I hung up when I heard his voice, shattered and shaken. One day I was working in the Plant Engineering office when he called. Matt was a young man who would hang out with me there. He seemed like a "mama's boy," soft spoken and chatty. Matt seemed to need a friend and never was a threat of any kind. The ringing of the phone interrupted our conversation. I answered the call, and the dreaded voice sounded on the other end of the line.

"I hope you are not calling it rape," he said.

I began to shake and handed the phone to my friend. "I can't make this guy stop calling me," I said, and dropped the phone in his hand.

What a surprise and relief when I heard my "namby-pamby" friend lay into him with threats of what would happen to him if he ever dared call me again. I couldn't believe the power in his voice and felt his protection calming me. My friend who I had believed to be like a lost child and seemed to have no friends or life of his own became my hero that day.

I never saw or heard from my rapist again. And I never told anyone about the rape. But what had happened to me on that night of horror had a long-lasting effect. Healing from the shame that buried itself deep in my psyche took years of sobriety and therapy. Drinking had made me vulnerable to the first rape. I don't remember drinking the night of this second violation. Nevertheless, both had been a shock to my system.

One day, not so long after this terrifying event, I decided to walk to work. It was a lovely day. I noticed there was a big black limousine that had slowed down and began to follow me. The driver rolled down the window and tried to sweet talk me into getting in the car with him. I couldn't understand what he was saying, and I dared not even look at him.

Then I heard, "Come on honey, try me. I'm a miracle."

I began to walk faster and thanked God I was almost at my destination. When I arrived at work, I was very shaken. As I told the people there what had just happened, they began to laugh and joke about how Joan had been accosted on the way to work. I didn't know whether to laugh or cry. They thought it was so funny. I had expected to get a hug from one of them and be reassured that everything was all right. That's not what happened.

"What's so funny? I asked. I felt angry, hurt, and wounded. I resented their lack of sensitivity. They just kept it up. I didn't get how they could think that it was funny. But then I slowly calmed down. Their humor helped me to relax. I began to see that nothing had actually happened to me, and my history of multiple rapes sensitized me to men who were predators.

"Who would get into the car with a sicko like that? Maybe it's not as threatening as I thought." I soothed myself with this notion. Nevertheless, I found a new route to work after that. The main street seemed safer. When winter arrived, I accepted a ride to work from a young man who worked at the university. He lived near me and offered to pick me up each morning.

But I wanted to continue to walk home so I could buy the evening bottle of booze. My rationalization was that it helped me sleep. Yes, I couldn't sleep unless I drank a pint of vodka. I was buying the lie that alcoholism told—a drink would always help me get through tough times.

Chapter 9—MIKE

Those Bonaventure years were the times when I got to know Mike. He came from Polish roots. When his grandfather arrived in America, the family settled near a Polish Catholic church in New Haven, Connecticut. The priest at the local parish needed an undertaker who was knowledgeable about Catholic beliefs to provide burial services to his parishioners when they died. When he asked Mike's grandfather if he would take the job, he agreed to get the necessary education. His grandfather served the community in this honorable profession for the rest of his life.

This marked the beginning of three generations of undertakers who provided service not only to the Polish people but the Slavic families in the area. Mike was the third and last generation involved in this family business.

Because they owned a limousine, Mike's family would pick us up and bring us from St. Bonaventure's to their home in New Haven, Connecticut. Those trips in the mortuary limousine were memorable.

The first time we visited, Father Gabe said Mass using the dinner table as an altar. Another time we all took a trip to the beach in the limo and had a wonderful day. When it was time to leave Connecticut, Father Gabe would head for his home in Massachusetts, and I traveled to mine Rhode Island.

There was so much activity in my life during those years, but Mike always helped me in one way or another. When I finally settled into my Bridgeport apartment, he visited the Newman Center often. Once, I asked a couple of the students if they knew any nice professors they could introduce me to. Their answer surprised me. They said I didn't need a professor because I already had an undertaker. I took it as a joke because I never thought of Mike as anything other than a kind friend. Besides, he was twelve years younger than I. At the time, I was thirty-four and he was twenty-two.

It wasn't long after that when Mike began asking me to marry him. I thought he was crazy because of the difference in our ages. Besides, he had one sister, and I had ten brothers and three sisters. He was Polish and had all kinds of Polish traditions. I was Irish and lived a very different life. These differences in our families and upbringing made for some communication gaps between us. We got some counseling from Father Gabe about getting married. He gave us many reasons why it might not work out between us.

After being raped in my own apartment, I began to see the difference between Mike and other men who were my age. He far exceeded them in quality and integrity. I realized what a wonderful man he was, and how good he was to me and for me. I felt safer with him and deeply respected by him. I finally said yes to his proposals of marriage.

Chapter 10—LIFE AS A WIFE

ℬ‍‍ℭℛℬ‍ℭℛℬ‍ℭℛ

Our wedding was to take place in the Newman Center. Father Devore, my co-chaplain, agreed to preside. The Newman kids were all planning to be there, as well as Mike's family.

My family couldn't attend. The day we picked up our marriage license was the day I found out Pa had died. My father died, and my mother had just buried him. I wasn't able to attend his funeral, but we put off the wedding for a few days. As a result, most of the college kids had already booked their flights home, so they didn't come to the wedding after all.

Mike; Joan; Maid of Honor, Janet; and Best Man, Tim

Mike's aunt approached me after we recited our vows. "Joan, I am very disappointed that you two lovebirds didn't get married in the

107

Polish church. I've always dreamed my little nephew would have a big, traditional church wedding."

She jarred me with her pronouncement. I answered her sincerely, "I'm so sorry. We never meant to disappoint you. We're not just young people starting out, so we thought a small ceremony would be better."

Her lower lip quivered a little. "It's just … it's just that I won't ever get to sing the solo at his wedding that I always dreamed of. I don't know if I can forgive you."

I was caught between the two competing emotions of grief and joy. I was happy with our wedding, but it shattered me when she told me how she felt. Having trouble forgiving me? Ouch! We left for our honeymoon the next morning. Mike's sister, his only sibling, drove us in the mortuary limousine to the airport.

We spent two weeks in a deluxe, newly built hotel in Bermuda. We did the usual—a little sightseeing, a little golf, and lounging on the white, sandy beach. Interspersed with relaxing, I drank and cried and grieved the loss of my father. It was such a bittersweet time—a mixture of deep sadness with joy and the excitement of being married and honeymooning in that exotic place.

Settling into our condominium in New Haven kept us busy. We were getting used to living together and focusing on making a nice home for ourselves. We decided that owning a dog would be a good idea, so we answered an ad for a young dog with characteristics of the husky breed. The couple who owned him were moving and couldn't take him with them. They lived in a woodsy part of town, so Gus was free to disappear into the woods. He came home when his master called him.

We were happy with our canine purchase, but to be honest, I knew nothing about caring for a dog. Living in a condo was quite different for Gus than living in a home backing up to the woods. He often ran away. He was hard to walk on a lead. He would steal food that had been left on the kitchen counter and take it into the bedroom to enjoy his feast on our beautiful new white bedspread. We had so much to learn about training a dog. So did Gus.

When I found out I was pregnant there was much joy in our family. At that time, we looked into buying a home. Before we found one, I had my first miscarriage around the end of the third month of the pregnancy. I was sad but didn't allow myself to grieve the loss properly. I got on with my daily chores and my job in an office—life went on. Soon afterward, I was pregnant once again, and we were all so happy once again, looking forward to the new addition to our family. I shopped for baby things and talked with my sisters and sisters-in-law on the phone about their children.

It was not to be. I lost the baby at the beginning of the fourth month. I still hadn't learned about working through loss, so I repeated what I did best—I got on with my life. I thought that was the right thing to do when adversity struck. Take the licks, get over it, and carry on. Any other reaction would be feeling sorry for myself.

When the third pregnancy appeared, I felt wary about my chances of carrying the baby to term. My concern was well-founded. I lost that baby also.

At the Yale School of Medicine, one of the physicians I consulted wanted to correct my bicornuate uterus. He believed it would improve my chances of carrying a child to term. Bicornuate means "having two horns." The normal uterus is pear-shaped, but the bicornuate uterus is heart-shaped with a dip in the middle.

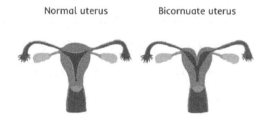

The physician explained the surgery would create a womb that was pear-shaped instead of split. It was supposed to be better able to carry a child to term. I underwent that surgery in the belief it would solve our problem. However, I continued to experience miscarriages. In the end, I had six miscarriages in the first five years of our marriage.

Although I drank less while I was pregnant, after six miscarriages, I had given up on having children and started drinking more. When I asked the Yale physicians why these six miscarriages had occurred, their only answer was that research into the matter was insufficient to answer my question. All they knew was that women with bicornuate uteruses, even if the malformation had been corrected, had a lower chance of carrying to term.

Next, we considered adoption. What a long and painful process adopting a child is. First, the adoption agency told us they had an infant who was up for adoption. When the woman doing the paperwork for this process noticed my age, we were refused the infant. She said it was their policy to give infants to younger mothers because it would be too difficult for someone my age to bring up a child from infancy. By this time, I was forty years old. The policy confused me because most women wouldn't give up on having their own children until they were my age.

Next, she suggested we adopt an older child who had a disability. I was infuriated and assumed an indignant stance, ready to fight the system. The people who loved me the most convinced me this was the wrong time to go to battle. I wasn't in top shape physically or mentally, as I was dealing with unresolved grief and physical exhaustion.

They were correct. I was mentally and physically exhausted from abusing alcohol and repressing my grief from the lost pregnancies. I didn't need much convincing to back down, so I put the idea aside.

I hadn't been attending Mass for several years. One morning, the thought struck me to go to daily Mass, where I might find something I had been missing. The priest at church, curious about my absence, asked if I had been on vacation. When I told him I'd had a series of six miscarriages back-to-back, he was stunned and so compassionate. He asked me how I handled so much loss. Of course, I thought he would be pleased when I announced I had just been "getting on with my life."

He seemed shocked at my impassive attitude. He had an office on the school campus and said he would be happy to offer me supportive counseling if I wanted it. His gentle caring grabbed my heart, and I found myself at his office quite often after that. The interesting thing about my counseling was that I found myself talking about a lot more than my miscarriages. Awareness of my innermost thoughts and feelings slowly grew after keeping them locked deep inside all my life.

Without realizing it, my psyche had been unraveling. My old, solid foundation of getting on with my life was corroding from the inside bit by bit. I'm not certain when my defenses began coming apart, but I knew the moment they collapsed.

When I became convinced I would never have a baby of my own, I left my job at the office and went back to the teaching profession. I worked in the office because I could leave it any time to be pregnant and care for my baby. Teaching was a full-time commitment. The new girl in the office could run circles around me in efficiency. My self-confidence was so diminished I had to do something that would restore my dignity and give me reason for being in this world.

Doing second-rate work in the office pushed me to tell my boss what I intended. He was surprised and concerned I intended to resume teaching. He thought it would be difficult for me to find a job in a school. Although his words undercut my confidence, I let him know I had a plan, and he shouldn't worry.

As a conciliatory gesture, I offered to throw the best Christmas party the office had ever had. This was my attempt at showing gratitude for his kindness while I was his employee. He was sad to see me go and concerned for me, but reluctantly agreed.

I liked my idea of beginning something new in the New Year. My first move was to meet the principal and some of the staff at the school two blocks down the street from where I lived. The principal and staff seemed warm and friendly. I offered to help any teacher who would accept my assistance, but, much to my surprise, no one took me up on it. I didn't ask for pay and was confused that teachers didn't want help from someone with a degree in education and experience teaching.

My motivation to work for free hinged on the fact that it had been some time since I taught school in Rhode Island. I was concerned that regulations there might be different from the Connecticut school system. I wanted to get the lay of the land, so to speak, and find out what I needed to know.

At last, a few teachers accepted me for tutoring a slow reader or two. The teachers and school administrators saw I was good with the students.

Very soon after, the principal offered me a job in the junior high school working with a small group of seventh graders who needed to catch up on their reading skills. I was so happy when I got this job. It was a government-funded program, and I only worked part time, which was perfect for me.

However, breaking into a new group of junior high school students was brutal. I took over in the middle of the year. The seventh graders didn't adjust easily to the change, especially since they had received no notice a new person would be taking over. I pulled out all that I had learned about rebellious pre-teens from my work at the orphanage, and we dug in with a new way of being with each other. I laid some ground rules and expectations and enforced the rules while showing them respect and compassion.

Once that was in place, we did some nice work together. At the end of that year, it warmed my heart when they threw me a party. They hung a sign which read:

TO A TEACHER WHO IS LIKE A MOTHER TO US

Seeing their sign warmed my heart, and I felt a nice bit of healing for the losses I had sustained.

Those years of teaching and growing into our marriage opened me up to a fresh world. We bought our home for quite a savings. We got a good deal because it had been the model home in a brand-new development, the showcase used to sell other people on moving into the subdivision. Getting to know our neighbors, experimenting with my gardening skills, throwing parties, and developing our own special circle of friends showed how our life was evolving.

My drinking was progressing also. I never even noticed it because everyone drank. It just seemed so normal and fun. Gradually it wasn't fun anymore. My hangovers were interrupting my weekends. I would miss church on Sundays nursing a hangover because I drank too much on Saturday night. When my weekend drinking moved into the weekdays, I became miserable.

Ten years into my marriage, I made it my mission to find out how to stop after one or two drinks. But that never worked. Once I started drinking, I continued drinking.

My next strategy was not drinking at all. At first, I could make it through a month sober. As time went by, my sobriety disappeared, and I drank every day again.

When I was drinking heavily, I called my friends and kept them on the phone for hours, telling them all about how hard my life was and all about my problems ... until I finally got the message—they didn't want to talk with me anymore.

My heart broke when I lost my friends. In my self-pity, I thought they were just cruel and had no compassion for my troubles. I had hit my lowest point, and had nowhere to go. It turned out to be a blessing in disguise when I couldn't turn to my friends because I turned to someone who could really help me.

I finally called someone who had given me her number long ago in case my brother ever reached out for help. He was at the height of his active alcoholism at that time. My brother eventually died of his disease, never asking for help.

Here it was years later, and yet I was hoping my friend would be able to help me with my own dilemma. I miraculously found her number. To this day I can't recall how or where I found it. When I called, I asked her if she knew how a person could get help with their drinking. She gave me some different ways to go about it and named a few rehabilitation facilities that might help. I had no idea what she was talking about. When she found out I was the one who needed the help, she seemed surprised. She set up a time for us to meet.

It was the beginning of a long, difficult journey into my sobriety. I learned a great deal about alcoholism and its effects. My behaviors and feelings of the past years began to make sense. I examined myself, my life, and my mistakes. I sought to make up for the wrongs I had done to others because of my drinking. Taking personal responsibility is of the essence, and I stayed the course of both physical and emotional sobriety. Once again, I moved into another new beginning after emerging beyond tragedy and confusion. This process of self-examination continues into the present.

One of the awakenings I had was that "when I was down to nothing, God was up to something." I kept discovering that God was doing for me what I could never do by myself.

The "something" God showed me included getting another master's degree that I would need to carry out my plan of loving service to others. In the healing process of change, we choose to move forward. When clearing space for grace, we can be open to other possibilities.

Chapter 11 — AWAKENINGS

ଛୠ୦୫ଛୠ୦୫ଛୠ୦୫

One of the greatest awakenings in my life was the insight that many of the pieces of my broken self served me well. I discovered that sobriety was an inside job that only I could do. I admitted the truth behind so many of the lies I had bought into and incorporated into my life.

Once I started taking responsibility for my choices, humble pie became everyday food. I ate that pie until I discovered that humiliation was quite different from humility. Humiliation filled me with shame, whereas humility set me free. Practicing sobriety taught me how to be free.

The journey into true sobriety is a walk into authenticity. It is a daily journey with a spiritual dimension followed by a choice to offer loving service to others. I made an incredible discovery that my true self had gotten lost. Every day I would find another piece of who I really was. And every day I became stronger as I persevered to find my truth. It is still so.

My horizons expanded, and I made an appointment with a Sister Rose, Registrar of

Albertus Magnus College in New Haven. I wanted to take a few courses in psychology to provide me with more guidance when I tried to help people who sought my counsel. She asked me to tell her my story.

When I finished, she leaned across her desk and said, "A few courses in psychology won't help you or those you want to help. The best thing for you to do is to apply to a master's program in counseling. Then you could wield some validity in the world of mental health services. Your circumstances are drawing you into this profession."

As Sister said this, she wrote on a piece of paper and handed it to me. On it was the name and number of a man she wanted me to call. This wise woman who had listened well to my long saga told me he was the head of the Department of Counseling at Southern Connecticut State University, and that I should tell him she had sent me. Sister Rose assured me that if I chose to follow up on her suggestion, he would get me into the right classes with the right teachers. From that comment I figured she would probably be telling him key pieces of my story.

My head spun as I walked out of her office. My hands shook, and I felt light-headed as I walked to my car. Looking around, it seemed as if I had been transported to another world. My heart skipped beats, and my mind raced.

I arrived home and sat at my kitchen table, praying for wisdom and guidance. My mind and heart slowly aligned as a measure of calmness returned—the direction came to follow her advice.

Joan and Mike at her graduation
for her master's degree in counseling

Chapter 12—SCHOOL DAZE

The counseling department at Southern Connecticut State University required that I take certain prerequisite courses before I could formally enter the master's program. I needed to complete some undergraduate courses in psychology and behavioral statistics before I could enroll in the graduate program.

I found it daunting to be among the young college students. They were all so open and assured, asking how I did on my first test. That test had me in a dither. I didn't even recognize the first question, never mind knowing the answer. The new subject matter required me to study in a different way than I did for my theology and education degrees. The multiple-choice questions required knowing the material in detail to find the correct answer. I'm not good at details, but I had to learn to memorize specifics.

My performance in the psychology class improved, but I wasn't doing well in statistics. My teacher suggested I work with a tutor, and recommended a young woman with good math skills. My complete lack of understanding of the material caused me considerable embarrassment, but my tutor was patient.

This young tutor was being treated for cancer. She was a beautiful young woman and extraordinarily kind. I found her ability to be present despite her health problems so moving. Her very life was threatened by a serious illness, yet when she helped me with my homework, she was there for me every minute.

We got along very well, and the results of her tutoring showed. My understanding of the coursework improved and my test scores increased. When the course was over, my professor congratulated my tutor and me because I passed my final exam. We both celebrated our success, and my gratitude for her wonderful help was lovingly received. I couldn't have done it without her help.

After a year, the prerequisites were out of the way, and my graduate studies began in earnest. My master's degree classes turned out to be a joy to me, and much less challenging than the undergraduate prerequisites. In many of the seminars, the students carried on class discussions and wrote papers on topics of our choice. The tests seemed easier because many of the questions were true or false.

I happily graduated with a Master of Science in counseling. As soon as I obtained my degree, I opened my own private practice. Once I had it all set up, I asked a friend who was a therapist working from her home, if she wanted to partner with me in the office. She seemed delighted with the idea.

We co-led some groups, and we each had a private office for our individual clients. It was a meager beginning, but as time went on our client caseload increased.

I found a bigger and better office suite right on the main road in town, in a Girl Scout office complex. The man who rented it to me loved what we were doing and was very encouraging and grateful for what we were all about. I named it the Center for Counseling, Recovery and Healing.

I also asked a massage therapist to join our

staff. Later on, an MD with a specialty in internal medicine who had chosen to move into the field of alternative medicine also joined us. To make this possible, we had a wall built to form another office area. The place was large enough so that even after doing this renovation, we still had waiting room space. I considered this continuing expansion such a gift that came from the One Who has all power and kept opening doors for me.

Chapter 13—INTENSIVE PSYCHOTHERAPY TRAINING

ഽറെഽറെഽറെ

I must confess that when I first started to see my clients, I noticed they needed more from me than the counseling I had learned in school. They were people who had been severely abused in many ways. They were quite literally trauma victims.

Because I knew they needed expertise beyond the scope of my practice, I asked a psychiatrist if he would evaluate and treat those who would benefit from medication in addition to counseling. He would also monitor those who were already on medications, often prescribed by their primary care provider. He graciously said yes. He and I used to meet for lunch on a regular basis to discuss each patient's treatment and how we could coordinate their care. What a gift this brilliant man was to me.

I hadn't learned everything there was to know about working with people with serious symptoms and set about getting educated in psychotherapy. The difference between counseling and psychotherapy is rather complex, but rests on psychological theory. Counseling is generally supportive in nature, using active or reflective listening techniques and empathy. Psychotherapy is based on psychological theories. Specific psychotherapeutic techniques are supported by scientific research, whereas counseling techniques are more general, and can't be tested scientifically.

The training group I joined was based in New York City and also used a cottage in Kent, Connecticut for what they called "Ten-Day Intensives." On Wednesdays, I would take a very early train into New York City to meet with a small group of psychotherapists at the Institute for Integrative Psychotherapy. This organization is still in existence, but has moved to Vancouver, Canada. The faculty is international.

Their treatment approach is called Integrative Psychotherapy because the founder, Richard Erskine, Ph.D., has found a way to combine almost a dozen theoretical approaches into one unified method of working with patients that affirms the value of the individual and taps into the spiritual dimension of life. Starting in the 1950s, the various theoretical orientations in psychology feuded among themselves about which one was best. In the 1980s, a movement to unite the different theories began, and Dr. Erskine's model was part of this movement.

Once or twice a year, I would drive to Kent, Connecticut to live with and learn from a large group of therapists from all over the world. For ten days, a lovely cottage in the historical town of Kent became our communal home. The leaders of the psychotherapy group owned the house and provided this peaceful setting.

A little lake in the back surrounded by beautiful flowers and trees took my breath away. These psychotherapists had been in the profession for years, and here I was—brand new in the field. It was a challenge for me at first, but I soon found myself learning so much from them, and my life seemed richer and flowed with joy and fulfillment once again.

I began using their techniques with my clients, and I saw how much they benefited from the strategies beyond supportive counseling. Once again, I had been led down the right path to provide loving service to the people who came to me for help.

Chapter 14—ANOTHER KIND OF RECONSTRUCTION

ഇരുഇരുഇരു

In the middle of my training in psychotherapy, I discovered I had breast cancer. In 1999, when my doctor discovered the disease, I was sixty-three years old. It was hard for me to believe I had cancer, because I had been taking such good care of myself, and my life was working out so well in my new profession.

Mike was more upset than I was. I helped him understand that I was unlikely to die from the kind of cancer I had. My goal was to take care of my body so I could continue to have a good life.

I had a large tumor in my left breast. Luckily, that type of cancer didn't spread to other parts of the body, but very often showed up in the other breast. I opted for removal of both breasts, using my own fat cells for the reconstruction. This technique is called "fat grafting." That meant I would also have a tummy tuck too when all was said and done.

I tried to help my husband understand the

diagnosis wasn't a death sentence. I was going to take care of this part of my body so I could continue a healthy life. Back then people would not even say the word "cancer." They called it the "Big C" with a look of fear and sense of impending death.

When the surgery was over, my cancer surgeon came to me in the hospital and told me I had made a good choice. The cancer had already invaded the other breast. I surprised everyone by getting out of bed quickly and left the hospital sooner than most.

I was still recovering from the surgery when I noticed something going amiss on the side where the cancer had started. The grafted fat didn't merge with my tissues properly and became necrotic, so it had to be removed. The dead fat cells left lumps in my breast.

In the end, I had to have a reconstruction of the reconstruction. The surgeon took fat cells from my back, and the end result didn't look natural. Because the new breast was smaller, I used a prosthesis to fill in the bra.

At that point I was just glad to be alive and

134

doing well after all the surgery. I felt very loved through this entire painful ordeal. The main ingredient for maintaining my wellness was the revelation of how much so many people loved me. They stepped into the role of my caretaker when I needed them. It was amazing and so *life-giving*. I use that word deliberately. Never underestimate the power of love. It is the ideal source for new life and inner healing.

After the surgery, I had several weeks of chemotherapy to kill any remaining cancer cells. During my chemo treatments, I listened to audio tapes of comedy performers. People would come into the room to find out what was so funny.

When I had my first chemo treatment, I expected to be weak and sick. When Mike came to take me home, I was delighted at how good I felt and danced my way to the car. What I learned was that it took a couple of days for the nausea to start. I could gauge which days were going to be more difficult than others. That gave me a chance to plan.

Most of my hair fell out when I was in the shower. I remember looking in the mirror afterward and saying goodbye to my hair. I had lustrous, dark hair and cried my goodbye.

After chemo, my wonderful oncologist advised me to have radiation treatment as a way to eliminate any remaining cancer cells. I balked at that, but in the end, I went back for the radiation treatments. To my surprise, I didn't have a problem with the radiation treatments at all. I was so happy to have my life back, dancing down the hall in the treatment center. When I was on the radiation table, I would smile at God and ask for His Divine radiation treatment to make me whole and holy.

During this entire cancer journey I had such generous friends showing up at my door to wash my hair, clean my house, cut up fruit for me, and even clean the tubes that were still draining the wounds from the surgery. I never felt so completely loved as I did through all of this.

I remember joking with Mike, "If I was not loved enough as a baby, this has more than made up for it."

When I returned to my psychotherapy

training group, I had lost all my hair. I decided not to bother wearing my wig anymore. The wig caused an itchy head, and I loved the comfort being bare-headed gave me. Once I learned to disregard the looks or comments from people who judged me for having no hair, I was fine.

Since my illness, I've been cancer free. There was some pain, but I received so much love, so much grace, and so many incredible memories.

The members of my psychotherapy training group loved my bald pate. They told me I had a nicely shaped head. I laughed and took delight in their comments. The people at church gasped and looked shocked, although once they found out I was all right, they were fascinated by the ringlets that grew in the back of my head.

I thought my hair would grow back curly, and that would have been just fine with me. Instead, it came back the same as before, only without any color—a stunning shade of silver. I loved it and also loved that not having it colored saved time and money.

I finished my training period in psycho-therapy and passed my performance session. I was now a certified Psychotherapist. All the trips to New York City and my Ten-day Intensives proved fruitful. It felt right and I had gained some valued professional psychotherapist friends. I continued to stay in touch with them and actually worked with one of the group's leaders as my own therapist. What a great decision I had made. I received the best therapy of my life for many years.

Chapter 15—BREAKDOWNS TO BREAKTHROUGHS

ಬಂಬಂಬ

Life in my marriage was becoming more difficult. My husband's increased drinking and subsequent alcoholic behaviors were creating a rift in our everyday lives. Losing the loving, thoughtful man who had brought me so much joy with his great sense of humor became more and more heartbreaking. I felt lonely in my own home. His behaviors became worrisome to me. What sustained me was having many friends and being able to give lots of loving service in my profession and in my church life. But being unable to share my life with Michael was unbearable.

Alcoholism is a lonely deteriorating and destructive disease, not only to the active alcoholic but to everyone in their life. I believed if Mike had gotten into a program of recovery, he would have thrived and re-connected with his true self. I loved him and wanted him to experience the love and caring he would receive, but it wasn't to be.

One night, Mike came home so drunk that he didn't know who he was or what he was doing. He babbled in a way I'd never heard from him before.

The bizarre behavior was frightening to me. After almost an hour, he fell into bed, quiet. I wondered if he had passed out. The next morning, he was gone before I awoke.

Worry about what would happen to him as his alcoholism progressed caused me to shake. I called him at work later that morning, holding the counter to steady myself against what I might hear on the phone.

His voice was calm. "Hello, Joan. What can I do for you?"

"You don't remember, do you Mike?"

He chuckled just a little, as if uncomfortable. "Remember what?"

I laid it all out for him. "You came in so drunk last night that you didn't know who I was or where you were. The things you were saying made so little sense that I can't even tell you what they were. You were babbling."

He started to interrupt, but I talked on.

"Mike, I'm so upset about this that my body is shaking. It's causing me stress. The doctor said too much stress might make my cancer come back, and I don't want that. I need to ask you for a separation, so I don't have to go through something like last night again."

Mike raised his voice on the phone, responding defensively, making it about him. "Look here, Joan. I did not cause your cancer. You can't blame that on me. I had nothing to do with you being sick, so knock that off right now."

I waited until he stopped yelling. His voice got quiet. "I think we should separate too."

I had expected an argument. His agreement surprised me. "Thank you for being so understanding, Mike. We can talk about it more when you get home."

After I hung up, I concluded he had given in so easily because he'd been having an affair. He knew seeing someone outside the marriage was hurting me. After we agreed to separate, he was very supportive of my needs and even helped me plan my trip to Florida with my friend.

Our marriage had become a charade, with both of us pretending to be man and wife. We were relieved the truth had been exposed that we were no longer partners and relieved to confess our mutual desire to live separately.

Mike came to me the next year. "Joan, I'm going to ask for a divorce."

I said to him, "All right, Mike. I think it's best."

He sat on the sofa in my apartment. "My friends tell me I'm crazy because I want to know if it's okay with you that I'm there when the sheriff comes with the papers."

I sat across the coffee table from him. "Mike, I'm glad that you want to be there to support me. I don't want the sheriff coming here to my apartment to do his presentation. Could we ask him to come to the funeral home.?"

Mike nodded. "Of course."

So, a few days later, we were at the funeral home. Mike stood next to me while the sheriff served me with divorce papers, and I accepted them. The sheriff left, and Mike put his arm around me. I put my head on his shoulder and cried.

"Mike," I sobbed, "I don't have my rosary beads with me."

He gave me a set from the stock he kept to wrap around the hands of the deceased as they lay peacefully in their coffins.

I took them, saying, "I'll get these back to you."

He patted my shoulder. "That's not necessary. You keep them."

We hugged and I left to go have a good cry in the chapel at the convent, where I prayed twice a week with the nuns. I was sad about no longer being married to Mike, at the same time knowing the divorce was long overdue. I would love Mike for the rest of my life.

He saw what was happening and knew he was on the brink of disaster. Out of love for me, he wanted to free me from any legal entanglements that would be left if he were to die.

We walked each other through the difficulties of the divorce. My lawyer was very pushy, believing Mike had more assets than he did, and she wanted to get what she believed I had coming so I could live comfortably. I asked her to back off, and I didn't get what she thought I should.

I took my family name back. He was happy for me when he found out I had gone back to McDermott. We stood on the courthouse steps hugging each other. Both of us wished the best for the other one. With great respect and the love we still had for each other, we said our goodbyes.

We had been married for thirty-three years. The very next year he died of a pulmonary embolism. On the way to the hospital the evening of his demise, he had asked his sister to tell me where he was. I never saw him alive again because Mike was dead by morning.

I was devastated when we lost him and thought I would never stop crying. It was a gut-wrenching period of deep grief that seemed endless. At the insistence of my niece and sister-in-law, I accepted their invitation to visit in California to rest and recover from all that had happened. My niece Therese and sister-in-law Muriel took me into their homes and their hearts during these visits. I experienced the love and caring that helped me through the worst days of grieving Mike's death and subsequently selling our home. A year after Mike died, I moved to California and made another new life on the heels of resolving the ravages of that grief.

Chapter 16—CALIFORNIA LIVING

Moving from the East Coast to the West Coast in 2009 made for an astonishing transition. I'm still adapting to all the changes. It took some time to get my own place, buy the furniture, and get settled with everything else I needed.

I chose my living quarters well. My apartment was called "a cottage on the lake." I must have had the best of all of the apartments in the entire complex. It was situated right on a lake, and I could see the swans glide by. They came onto the shore right where I lived. In the spring and summer, watching the sail boats and canoes and rowboats was sheer heaven to me.

The country club next door rented paddle boats that the college students had such fun with. My outside deck gave me a place to relax on nice days where I could watch the activity. I set up feeders for hummingbirds and all kinds of other engaging bird visitors. The ducks found a way of getting under the fence that separated our property from the water. They came to eat the bird seeds and anything else that they could find beneath the feeders.

My apartment had two bedrooms and a bath to go with each. I loved having guests, and for a while I housed one of the exchange students from the University of California at Davis. The beautiful view from the guest bedroom window was spectacular. One of my regular guests used to call the time spent with me "time at the Hilton."

While making my bed in the morning I took great comfort in my own gorgeous lake view. The swans glided in the water, while the geese flew in formation to other lakes in the area. It was a sad day when I had to leave. The rent rose to an amount beyond my means, and I was afraid to commit to another year and find I wouldn't be able to pay.

During the time I lived there, I took a class on memoir-writing. I discovered something baffling while writing those stories of my history. I took the subject the instructor gave us to write about, think of a memory that would speak to it, and write effortlessly. My fingers flew over the keys.

After we finished, class members would read what they had written to the class. Each one of us always produced a surprising piece of composition. I really loved writing and reading my stories to the class.

Another discovery once the classes ended was that my memories brought me sweet healing. I had been grieving the loss of Mike and my home and the friends I had left behind. This vehicle of expression of the happier memories along with the sadder ones brought a sense of closure and wholeness to my life. I daresay, in writing this book you are now reading, I am once again experiencing the transformational power of writing from my heart and soul.

Since living as an inhabitant of the West Coast here in California, I've had to navigate many transitions. I love my life here and appreciate the beauty of nature from this side of the country. I still miss the enchanting autumns and the incredible Atlantic Ocean of the East Coast. After I decided to stay here permanently, I used to go back east each October to catch the beauty of the foliage. I would rent a car and visit my friends. Each trip to a different friend's home gave me ample time to soak in the gift of delightful scenery on the way.

During the years I have lived here, my niece Therese was an integral part of every decision and move that I made. She and my favorite

Muriel and Joan (right)

sister-in-law Muriel, my brother Frank's wife, became a great source of joy and comfort for me.

Back home in Providence, Rhode Island, Muriel worked in the ice cream parlor across the street from the playground . When I was a little girl, my mother would send me to Jenny's Ice Cream parlor to buy her favorite treat—a quart of coffee ice cream. The bell rang when I walked through Jenny's door. Muriel looked up, smiled at me, and asked for my order. She always made me feel so important. She had me sit down and treated me to an ice cream cone while she filled the order.

The first time I came to visit her in California, she had that same big, welcoming smile. She spoiled me right from the start by inviting me to drink a cup of tea. We sat and chatted for a while. Once again, I fell under the spell of her loving attention. I lived in her home during those visits. It was because of Therese and Muriel that I was able to see more of California than I could ever have on my own.

To lose my sister-in-law after I moved to California made me sad. She died during

Therese's cancer journey. Therese and I spent some sweet time with Muriel before she passed on. One day she was sitting in her lounge chair, and I began singing in her ear. She started singing with me. Therese got the camera and took photos. Those were such sacred moments. That evening Muriel died peacefully.

Therese seemed to be doing well after the stem cell implantation surgery, but her cancer came back, metastasized to her bones. After that

Neice Therese

it was touch and go. The cancer spread up the spinal column into her brain, and she died shortly after.

Therese's death was a significant loss to me. I am forever grateful that her husband made sure I got to the hospital to say goodbye before she left this world.

Later her husband told me she asked him to make sure I visited her before she passed. Therese's loving nature was a gift to us all, especially me.

Chapter 17—FROM ENDINGS TO BEGINNINGS

ೋೀೋೀೋೀ

So many things happened after Muriel and Therese passed away. I didn't have the credentials to practice psychotherapy in California because they are very strict about licensing, but I could be a life coach. My new life coaching practice was just taking off.

I invested in a promotional program that I believed would be an enormous boost to the growth of my practice. Unfortunately, I had agreed to a program that cost thousands of dollars. I thought the cost was hundreds, which I could handle at that time. I also thought it would be smart to put it on an automatic payment plan. Later, I discovered what was going on and worked to get it straightened out. But the money the company took from my accounts left me in debt, and I could no longer stay where I was living because I couldn't afford the rent. I needed new housing.

At the very last minute I discovered a newly built government-funded housing complex for seniors and disabled folks. Because of its newness, there was no waiting list. I filled out all the paperwork required and was accepted. I had to be out of where I was by the end of August, which was only a few weeks away.

One evening when I went for my stroll, I couldn't walk straight, I felt lightheaded, and I felt pressure inside my head. I prayed my way through the last block to my apartment, made my dinner, and went to bed thinking I would feel better in the morning. During a Zoom meeting at 6:30 a.m., I noticed on the computer monitor that my mouth looked crooked. *What if I've had a stroke?* I thought.

After the meeting, one of my friends assured me she would come to my home and pick me up. All I needed to do was get ready, and she would take me to the emergency room.

I had indeed experienced a mild stroke. This happened mid-August. I still had to move, but the new place hadn't finalized my acceptance. A wonderful lady I knew from the Zoom meeting offered me a place to stay until I could make the move to my new apartment.

These circumstances with the stroke and moving were so disruptive to me, but I had friends who wanted to help me. I kept my innermost being as balanced as possible and let them do their thing. They packed my belongings on a truck and placed them in a storage unit.

Because I was recovering from the stroke, all I could do was to sit and watch this self-formed team work in such an orderly fashion that was so impressive to me. It filled me with gratitude. My personal bags were packed, and friend took me to her lovely home. I spent a couple of weeks with my friend. Staying with her was so good for me. She was so gentle and kind and had a great sense of humor. The kindness of others saved me again.

When I got word that I could move into my new apartment, my friends and I packed up my belongings. The gracious lady who had taken me into her home now took me to my new apartment. Exhausted, I just wanted to get settled into my home. Before I received my key, we had to sit for an hour and listen to the rules and regulations. My friend took notes on them.

She was such a blessing to my impatient, resentful, and weary heart.

When we finally got to the apartment, I was anything but grateful. While turning the key in the door, I complained to myself that it was like walking into a prison. My friend, on the other hand, seemed overjoyed at what she was seeing. The apartment was roomy and brand new. An outside deck embellished the sunny side of the building.

I was too wrapped up in my own bitterness and resentment to share her joy. A week passed before I realized how blessed I was to have a home, especially one this comfortable. The scales fell away from my eyes, and I saw the favor of God in all that had transpired. Feeling so much love and the realization of the incredible help I had been given, replaced my feelings of resentment.

A week after I arrived, I fell on the walkway into the office. I fractured my left arm near the shoulder and incurred other injuries in a hard fall. I ended up in an inpatient physical therapy rehabilitation program for almost a month. After becoming more physically active and returning to my apartment, my friends helped me unpack boxes and hang pictures on my walls.

My badly fractured arm became more usable with outpatient physical therapy. It took some time, but I made good progress. Soon I became more able to do things that in the past had been so simple and easy for me. I became steadier on my feet and able to take walks outside using the walker that had been a gift to me from an anonymous friend. I took a walk on the greenbelt that began at the end of the apartment property. Life began to seem more doable. But I still have small bouts of vertigo and experience numbness in my left leg. I still find it takes longer to get dressed, especially getting my shoes on.

I had been so miserable for a while, crying the blues about all I had lost. The stroke and losing the ability to move my body easily because of the fall had seemed so debilitating. Besides that, the government wouldn't let me make money with life coaching or any other way if I lived in a government-subsidized complex.

The final straw was choosing to sell my car. The stroke made me think twice about driving. Besides, I needed the money to help me pay my debts.

Thinking about all this loss dragged me into a place of self-pity and even worse, self-criticism for all I had done to bring this upon myself. This particular type of negative self-obsession was the most disturbing of all. Self-hatred is deadly. My mind was definitely a house divided against itself. I was losing hope and didn't dare dream of a happy future. Everything seemed so bleak and dark and hopeless. I had lost so much self-confidence.

Earlier I wrote about awakening. That isn't something that happens once in a person's lifetime. We fall back to sleep into ignorance and awaken to our truth over and over. I awoke to the damage that this kind of negativity causes. It wreaks havoc on body, soul, mind, and spirit. I made a deliberate choice to live in an attitude of gratitude, to redeploy joy. I chose to be grateful for all that I had instead of complaining about all I had lost.

This kind of change is accomplished one step at a time. First, I began to live by choosing joy at each segment of the day, morning, noon, and evening. Then, I set about making my new home a place of sweetness by welcoming all who came to my door.

This was going on just when the Covid pandemic erupted. Because of my inability to go places and do outside things, I didn't feel much change from the isolation imposed by Covid-19. I had already been isolated for other reasons. Still, it seemed like such a long road ahead before I could be productive. Undeterred, I committed to my resolution, and a day at a time, I began to feel a change in me.

Once again, I discovered that on the other side of loss is new life. I am happy to say that now I love being able to walk with my walker the entire length of the green belt that begins at the edge of our apartment complex property. It takes me all the way to Target and a few other stores in a little mall. Walking brings me great joy and a measure of independence. My heart sings as I walk along every day. I have also changed my eating habits. I am feeling healthy, wealthy, and wise—and loving it.

Mark Nepo's *The Book of Awakening* has a subtitle I really relate to. It states, *Having the Life You Want by Being Present to the Life You Have.* What Mark Nepo means is being present in each moment of your life rather than thinking of the things that have happened to you in the past or worrying about the things that might happen to you in the future. Every moment we spend reviewing our past regrets is wasted, and every moment we spend worrying about things that have yet to happen, and most likely never will, is wasted.

He doesn't mean not to plan for the future by budgeting our money or buying insurance. He means to be present in each moment of your life and to live it fully. We can notice the beauty all around us and spend our moments adding to the beauty that is already there by arranging flowers, making our bed, or smiling at a stranger.

This way of living brings strength and joy to my spirit. As a consequence, it also brings healing to my mind and body. Life is good these days, and I am up to any challenge. Because of clearing space for grace, I find by letting go of what was, I am able to embrace open-heartedly what is in the now of each moment of each new day.

In the writing of this book, I have been transported to the clarity of my core message. On the other side of a loss of any kind, we can find new life in our new beginnings. The grieving process is actually the clearing space for the grace of a power greater than ourselves. It reveals to us the depth of who we really are. The Spirit of Life itself breathes hope, help, and healing into the broken places deep in our souls. It happens over the span of our lifetime as we uncover, discover, and recover our authentic selves.

EPILOGUE

I pray you will take what belongs to you from my story telling. I pray you will be inspired by what I call my Divinely choreographed life, and also laugh at some of my shenanigans. Most of all, I pray you will come to know that you can trust the process of grieving, as difficult and heartbreaking as it is. Grief's resolution holds the door open to create a new life without losing the best of what was. I continue to cherish the sacredness of my past even as I let go of the pain suffered. My authentic self is inextricably one with the Source of all energy. I call that Source the Divine within, the infinitely loving God of my heart. I have found that grief's resolution flows from that power of Divine love.

I can see more clearly now. I had lost my way and needed to recapture my true north. On my business cards a few years back, I had printed, "Sometimes in the winds of change we find our true direction." I meant it as a reassurance for my clients, but it applied to me as well.

The essence of this saying captures the feeling that has been building in me over this past year. I have dropped into my deepest soul, and in the space of grace, I am more able to own all of me. I am practicing every day what grief now teaches me.

1. Embrace all my fears. They are my best teachers.
2. Renew my precious relationship with my sacred innermost self.
3. Know I am unconditionally loved and energized by the purity of Divine love.

This is the way I have found to become whole, integrated and authentically me. This pure energy is infiltrating the recesses of my being as I open up each day to its power. This is the God of my heart and soul—The One I fell in love with as a child. I will be undergoing this process for as long as I am able to breathe. I will surrender to Divine Love.

REFERENCES

Beatty, M. *The Language of Letting Go: Daily Meditations for Codependents.* Center City, MN: Hazelden Publishing, 1990.

Nepo, M. *The Book of Awakening: Having the Life You Want by Being Present to the Life You Have.* San Francisco: Red Wheel/Weiser, LLC, 2000.

"The Peace Prayer of St. Francis," Author unknown. French version from 1912. Retrieved from https://www .franciscan-archive.org/franciscana /peace.html. April 25, 2022

AUTHOR BIOGRAPHY

R. Joan McDermott lives in Northern California after moving there from New England where she'd lived since birth. Her journey has taken her from a consecrated life as a

Sister of Mercy to a married woman to a psychotherapist. Along the way, Joan discovered she had become an alcoholic, and  found a way to get sober and stay that way through her spirituality.

In her memoir, she details her journey and reveals the key to integrating and elevating the secular with the spiritual life—feeling gratitude and clearing space in one's life to admit grace.

PLEASE LEAVE A REVIEW

ഇൗരുഇൗരുഇൗരു

Self-published authors thrive on reviews. Please write a few words on the book's Amazon page or on Goodreads, describing what you thought of Joan's memoir.